A Good
Apology

A Good Apology

Four Steps to Make Things Right

MOLLY HOWES, PhD

GC

GRAND CENTRAL
PUBLISHING

NEW YORK   BOSTON

Copyright © 2020 by Mary J. Howes, PhD
Cover design by Lisa Amoroso. Cover copyright © 2020 by Hachette Book Group, Inc.

Grand Central Publishing
Hachette Book Group
1290 Avenue of the Americas, New York, NY 10104
grandcentralpublishing.com
twitter.com/grandcentralpub

First Edition: June 2020

Grand Central Publishing is a division of Hachette Book Group, Inc. The Grand Central Publishing name and logo is a trademark of Hachette Book Group, Inc.

The publisher is not responsible for websites (or their content) that are not owned by the publisher.

The Hachette Speakers Bureau provides a wide range of authors for speaking events. To find out more, go to www.hachettespeakersbureau.com or call (866) 376-6591.

Library of Congress Cataloging-in-Publication Data

Names: Howes, Molly, author.

Title: A good apology : four steps to make things right / Molly Howes, PhD.

Description: New York : Grand Central Publishing, 2020. | Includes bibliographical references and index. | Summary: "Dr. Molly Howes uses her own experiences with patients at her practice to exemplify the importance of a proper apology, and how we can all hone our technique. Learn how to craft an effective apology with this four-step model: 1. Listen to and empathize with the other person's hurt 2. Make a sincere statement of regret and acknowledge harmful actions 3. Make restitution for the pain caused 4. Prevent repetition of the injury An apology is a small-scale event between people, but it's enormously powerful. Never until now has there been a comprehensive book giving readers the tools to fix their relationships, make amends, and move forward, all through the power of a great apology"-- Provided by publisher.

Identifiers: LCCN 2019050663 | ISBN 9781538701317 (hardcover) | ISBN 9781538701324 (ebook)

ISBNs: 978-1-5387-0131-7 (hardcover), 978-1-5387-0132-4 (ebook)

Printed in the United States of America

LSC-C

10 9 8 7 6 5 4 3 2 1

To the courageous people who've sat with me
and shared their stories,
I dedicate this gift of gratitude.

Contents

Contents

INTRODUCTION

I am perhaps obsessed with apologies. As a psychologist, I find them crucial in my work with people. I pore over books on the subject and study religious texts. For years, I've collected apology stories. I clip them from newspapers, old-school style, and keep them in a box under my desk.

Recently, the stack has grown fast.

During the #MeToo movement, we've watched the march of shame across our newsfeeds by high-profile men accused of sexual misconduct. The examination of apologies has become a national pastime and given "I'm sorry" the weight of a political act. Whether they are from heads of state who relay their official remorse for governmental mistreatment of citizens or from well-known figures in front of microphones who regret their deception, sexual misconduct, and other trust-breaking behavior—we tweet and post, debate and dissect the sincerity and effectiveness of these public statements. We've made such a sport of apologies that the *New York Times* has presented us with a "Choose Your Own Public Apology" column with fill-in-the-blank options.[1] For all our public dialogue, however, the apologies themselves don't seem to be getting much better.

Right now, we are in an extended moment of public attention focused on saying "I'm sorry," but the value of apologies is timeless and universal. We need good ones in our personal lives every bit as much as we need them in public discourse. Each time we face another person's injury with courage and humility, we heal individual hurt. When we apologize, we restore damaged connections. We reduce our isolation and shame, and we make our relationships stronger. We build a kinder and more civil society.

So, if apologies are so useful and important, why are we so bad at them?

Of the hundreds of patients I've worked with, many struggle with how to apologize well—as do many of the people I know outside my practice. I, too, have missed opportunities and made my share of poor attempts to repair mistakes. For a myriad of cultural and psychological reasons, apologizing well is really hard to do. Human perceptual and cognitive biases make seeing our own mistakes and their effects on other people challenging. Most of us labor under misconceptions and myths about apologies, including the idea that our intentions determine our effects on other people. That is, if I didn't mean to hurt you, you can't be hurt. Or we subscribe to the now-historic Hollywood notion that "love means never having to say you're sorry." Further, we rarely see public figures modeling good apologies.

Many of us make no attempt to apologize when we should, and when we do, it's often in ways that inflame the situation or, at best, only partially heal the damage. But the good news is that each of us has the capacity to make an effective apology. One of the biggest, most universal roadblocks is a simple lack of technique. That's why I wrote this book.

* * *

Introduction

My journey toward developing an apology technique began in childhood. In the face of chaos and neglect, including three years I spent in an orphanage, I did what children often do: I tried to control what I could control. When I couldn't fix the unpredictable world around me, I learned to mend physical things. I replaced errant buttons and glued shattered dishes back together. Even as a child, I had trouble tolerating waste. I held on to broken things long before I learned that relationships, too, can be salvaged rather than discarded.

Although I was unaware of it at the time, that early effort was good preparation for becoming a psychologist. My faith that hurt can be repaired undergirds my approach to psychotherapy as well as my personal philosophy. I serve as a "hope merchant." I can see possible favorable outcomes, and I can help people journey through thorny terrain to reach them.

Earlier in my career, though, I was at a loss when grappling with the unresolved cracks between people. Just out of college, I worked with a woman who lived in extreme isolation because she couldn't face the family she'd "let down way too many times." I was puzzled and frustrated that she didn't respond to her family's attempts to connect with her, but I didn't know how to help her move through her shame. Months later, she killed herself. I'll never forget the stunning sense of wastefulness I felt. Her life was lost because she couldn't face and mend what she'd damaged.

Soon after, in graduate school, I worked with a couple who'd spent almost three decades unhappily stewing about the husband's flirtation with another woman during their first pregnancy. I could teach them to communicate better, but I didn't know yet how to help them face their stubborn resistance and resentment so that they could heal this foundational wound.

Throughout my training, I met other couples stymied by hurt they couldn't get past and individuals who were as troubled by their own harmful behavior as they were wounded by others'. Psychotherapy usually addresses a person's internal experience of hurt, not the pain or guilt from having hurt other people. I found no supervisor I could turn to or book I could consult that focused on the problem of addressing one's own responsibility for mistakes and wrongdoing.

Again and again, I saw how unhealed hurt between people hardened into bitterness and judgment. I saw how unprocessed guilt darkened into chronic shame and low self-esteem. I saw how rifts between people seemed impossible to reach across and so resulted in unhappiness and loneliness. At its worst, failing to mend relationships led to dangerous levels of isolation.

Public health research suggests that weak social connections can be as harmful to a person's life span as heavy smoking and more damaging than obesity. The social and emotional support our close relationships provide improves everything from stress management to lung function[2] and coronary heart disease.[3] Despite the value of relationships to our physical and psychological health, many people do not have or maintain them. In 2018, the United Kingdom appointed its first minister for loneliness to address the needs of the many British citizens who report that they are often or always lonely.[4] In the United States, up to 40 percent of Americans over the age of forty-five suffer from chronic loneliness.[5] Vivek Murthy, the former US surgeon general, referred to loneliness as "a growing health epidemic."[6]

In the 1980s, during my clinical fellowship at Harvard Medical School, I began to encounter ideas that would eventually lead to my apology model. My training occurred during a time of transformational thinking in psychology. New, field-changing research findings challenged Lawrence Kohlberg's long-dominant theory that a person reached the height of morality when he or she acted according to "universal ethical principles" (a set of internalized, abstract codes of conduct). Carol Gilligan, who had worked at Harvard with Dr. Kohlberg, published her now-famous findings that women held themselves to different standards than the male subjects Dr. Kohlberg had mainly studied. Her female subjects evaluated whether an action was right or wrong according to whether it harmed or helped another person—what Dr. Gilligan called an "ethic of care."[7] Morality was not purely an interior, individual phenomenon, but also a social one based in our connections to others.

At the same time, the theory of self psychology was taking the psychoanalytic world by storm. Psychiatrist Heinz Kohut, a refugee from Nazi Austria, developed a model in which the therapist had to be radically empathic for any hurt the patient experienced in the course of therapy. He argued that the hurt was real and healing it could lead to important progress. The therapist's task was to listen and empathize in order to help the person heal.[8]

This was also the era when psychiatrist Jean Baker Miller and her colleagues at Wellesley College's Stone Center for Research on Women formulated new understandings of both psychological development and psychological health, ones that centered around connections between people. Their "relational" model challenged the conventional understanding that the goal of human development was individuation and that most other people could be considered potential competitors.[9]

These ideas provided the clinical guideposts I followed in my exploration of how relationships hurt and heal us. Along the way, I became fascinated by the radical courage and care that seemed necessary for mending damaged connections. Across decades, in thousands of hours of psychotherapy sessions, I began to see openings, opportunities for brave souls to recognize an injury they'd caused and to reach across a chasm of hurt toward someone on the other side. With growing hope that interpersonal pain might be reparable, I asked about those possibilities more directly. An estranged daughter recognized that, in addition to her father's "fault" for their difficulties, her unkindness had contributed to their rift. A patient spoke about his friend's perspective on a recent conflict between them.

Introduction

Breaches often could be approached and sometimes mended. I learned first to recognize and then to encourage steps that repaired hurt between people. A husband could suddenly stop his counter-complaints against his partner and offer a sincere apology. A woman considered ways to make up for having missed her angry sister's birthday celebration. A couple tried to rebuild trust after unfaithfulness.

In contrast to the dark and lonely outcomes from avoiding an apology or the messy blowback from an inadequate one, I witnessed a deep spiritual lifting of burdens and an opening of hearts when people faced a previous hurt with courage and humility. Their relationships didn't just recover; they grew stronger.

An apology may be a small-scale event between people, but it's enormously powerful. We've all done something wrong or made a mistake or insulted someone—even if by accident. We've all been hurt and wanted the other person to help us heal. Maybe you've experienced a family disagreement that didn't get resolved and resulted in painful distance between siblings or with your parents or children. Maybe you've suffered the tension of unaddressed resentment with your partner. Maybe a dear friend is no longer so close because of an injury that seemed too uncomfortable to talk about. Or perhaps you're one of the millions of Americans staring across a cultural or political gulf at your loved ones on the other side, feeling uncertain and hurt. Aside from actual abuse situations, these circumstances can be faced and fixed.

It is counterintuitive, perhaps, but the breaches themselves aren't the real issue; our inability to fix them is what causes us trouble. It's the failure to learn from one another and our missteps that keeps us from developing the resilient relationships we long for and need. We don't really require a study or government official to show us that failure to mend breaks in relationships with partners, children, siblings, parents, colleagues, and friends hurts us in all kinds of ways. What we haven't understood is how to fix the problem. Until now.

Introduction

So, what words and deeds actually repair broken trust and heal us, our relationships, and our societies? What, essentially, *is* a good apology? I've written this book to answer that question.

Based on decades of clinical work, and incorporating religious tradition, legal thought, social justice concepts, and psychological science, I developed a four-step model of apology that's accessible and straightforward. The technique is informed by research that has studied people as varied as high-performing CEOs and incarcerated criminals, the science of how often humans make mistakes, and observations of how our brains operate under stress. Perhaps equally important, it's based on commonsense actions that you don't have to be an expert to take. I don't mean to say that apologizing is a piece of cake. But there is a way to make amends that leaves everyone feeling better.

Spelled out in simple steps, my model will show you how to understand the other person's hurt, to express your regret, to make the harm right, and to prevent it from happening again.

In *A Good Apology: Four Steps to Make Things Right*, you will see real people's brave efforts to make repairs to damaged relationships, across many spheres of life and many types of connections. You may be most interested in

- how to heal a relationship with another person,
- how to resolve family conflicts,
- how to mediate conflicts so business teams work better,
- how to heal breaches due to divisive political disagreements,
- how to best contribute to social justice work, or
- how to teach children to make better, more real apologies.

No matter where your interests lie, *A Good Apology* will help you understand why it's so important to apologize, as well as why it's so hard. Stories of personal attempts to mend relationships, along with compelling research findings, will illustrate the positive power of the four-step apology model. Within relationships, these steps can rectify wrongs, reduce resentment, salvage connections, and foster greater intimacy. For yourself, they can ease shame, enhance self-esteem, and make you a healthier and happier person. Ultimately, you can cultivate an attitude of more compassionate accountability, that is, holding yourself and others responsible for missteps while maintaining a kind and humane approach to the important people in your life.

A Good
Apology

PART I

APOLOGIZING IS TOO HARD TO DO AND TOO IMPORTANT *NOT* TO

CHAPTER 1

Why Apologize?

A good apology can be an intimate effort or an international exchange. Its importance lies both in its immediate effects and in its long-lasting impact on a relationship of any kind—friendship, marriage, family, nations, or institutional, religious, or ethnic groups. Not only does an effective apology restore balance to a relationship, it changes patterns and creates new possibilities. Every successful resolution builds on the benefits of previous ones, but, by the same token, after every missed chance to repair harm, the costs add up. Not having a workable way to say "I'm sorry" to the relevant person(s) can lead to long cycles of mistrust and conflict. For an individual, righting a wrong creates better psychological and spiritual health, whereas the buildup of guilt that isn't expiated becomes a burden for the spirit. Within relationships, a failure to make amends can set in motion negative patterns of resentment and distance.

When Lisa and Philip sat in my office at our first meeting, the space between the two red armchairs they occupied seemed to expand into leagues of distance. They didn't look at each other and didn't address each other. Their presenting problem was near-constant bickering, which they readily reproduced for me, even while referring to the other in the third person. Their habitual arguing rarely led to conclusions. Irritable, unsatisfying exchanges had become their primary form of conversation.

Lisa and Philip were both in their midthirties, each with a wide circle of friends, steady connections, large families, and generally satisfactory jobs. Originally, they had planned to have children but hadn't been able to reach a decision about actually starting a family. Recently, when the word "divorce" came up in an argument, it had scared them both into seeking therapy. They were genuinely mystified about how they'd landed in this frustrating, distant marriage.

I asked about the beginning of their relationship, before they'd gotten married four years earlier. They both brightened. Philip described their shared pleasure in bowling and line dancing.

As he spoke, Lisa smiled and, almost interrupting him, spoke to him for the first time in my presence: "Yeah, remember when we discovered we liked to do the same dorky things?"

He nodded and they told me, *in unison,* "It was great!"

For a moment, we all sat silent. Their striking shift, from very distant to quite united, was unmistakable.

I asked them when things had changed. Neither knew, but tension crept back into both their voices as they described the beginning of their married years.

Lisa: "We couldn't agree about anything, even where to hang pictures."

Philip quickly followed with, "Yeah, she always criticized how I did it."

"He never asked for my opinion before he went ahead and drove in a nail."

He scowled and spoke to her: "You never volunteered to help, did you?"

"I can use a hammer, too. But you never included me."

"Did you really care about the pictures?"

"No, Phil, I really didn't care." Her voice dropped. "I really *don't* care."

A heavy, unhappy silence. Then, to me, Lisa said with a sigh, "I finally gave up and let him do it however he wanted."

"But she never stopped complaining about it."

I intervened. "This sounds like an argument you've had before, maybe not just about the placement of artwork."

Philip: "All the time."

Lisa: "If we're talking at all."

Philip: "Yeah, we just stop talking after a while. The arguments don't really end."

Lisa, more slowly: "I've just never understood why we can't have things between us the way they were before we got married." The couple had been together for several years before their marriage and had happily spent most of their free time together.

Each aspect of their married life seemed to reflect the same maddening motif: Each time they encountered conflict, they eventually gave up without resolution. Frustration and resentment grew.

The more I inquired about the change in their relationship, the more Lisa fidgeted and twisted Kleenex in her hands. When Philip mentioned their wedding itself, she held her right hand in front of her eyes. Tears ran slowly down her cheeks. Philip turned to me and shrugged, puzzled. Her unhappiness was palpable, but neither of them could tell me what she was crying about.

They agreed to return. I framed our task as trying to understand the puzzle of what changed for them and whether it had something to do with their wedding.

In our next sessions, Lisa could only cry and cover her face at first, embarrassed by such strong feelings. Over time she began, haltingly, to relate pieces of their wedding weekend. Finally, she articulated her painful disappointment with how Philip acted, especially on the night of his bachelor party. He'd returned to the hotel disheveled and smelling of perfume. As she related, she had tried to talk with him about it late that night as well as the following morning, but he'd been inebriated and hungover, respectively. Both times he'd been irritated by her questions. At the wedding reception, there had been much laughing and smirking among the groomsmen, and Lisa had grown increasingly unhappy. On their honeymoon, she'd brought up the subject again, but he had waved off her concerns, telling her not to be ridiculous.

In my office, Philip listened silently to her story, but when she stopped, he finally burst out with, "You've been holding a grudge all this time? Why didn't you say something?"

Lisa was visibly taken aback by his question and answered slowly that she just now realized she'd avoided even thinking about their wedding for years. She pointed out that she'd never ordered wedding photographs and had given away her dress.

Philip shook his head slowly. "Wow."

"Yeah, ever since, at our friends' weddings, I think I always drink too much."

"You think?"

"Yes." She ignored his sarcasm. "And I usually stay as far away from Philip as possible."

Another silence as that sad realization sank in.

"So, you argue with me about everything but don't talk to me about this." Philip's accusation had a bitter edge, the feeling that comes from finding out you might be blamed for something you'd been unaware of.

I stepped in. "You may be right, Philip. Maybe that's *why* you fight about everything else." Their habit of squabbling seemed to develop as a sort of placeholder for communication they hadn't been able to have. It was the indication that things were not good between them, but, like many such relationship warnings, it presented itself in an unknown language.

I continued, "What about this old hurt, though? You two never healed it, never even had a conversation about it. It began like a small infection and stayed, untreated, in your system."

"So, what now? What can we do now?" Still perturbed, Philip turned toward his wife and said, "So I'm supposed to tell you I'm sorry after all this time?"

She shrugged slowly, at a loss.

Earlier in my career, I might have agreed that the opportunity for apology had long ago passed and that our task was to help Lisa move on. But by the time I met Philip and Lisa, I knew that it's never too late to apologize. Bad relationship habits may have damaged the bond between people, but if you have a sincere wish to repair harm in your relationship, it's always worth trying to have the conversation. In this case, even though Philip was upset that he'd been in the dark, both partners were eager to find a way to fix their problematic patterns.

"Yes," I responded to Philip's question, "an apology is exactly what we need to do." They had never healed the old hurt. "Let's figure out how to do it together."

I see their problem as resembling a physical wound. Medical advice for treating cuts or surgical sites has changed since I was a child—even since my children were young. Rather than letting the skin dry out ("let it breathe," we used to say) and form a scab, the recommendation is to keep the wound moist, so it can heal from the inside. Now it's believed that if the outside closes up prematurely, it can seal in an infection and the injury ultimately will heal less well. Now we are advised to promote what's called "wet wound healing." That's one way of understanding what happens when a needed apology is missed. The bleeding may have stopped, but the wound hasn't really healed. To keep the subject open until it's dealt with leads to more genuine healing.

I should point out here that Philip wasn't avoiding an apology all these years. Neither of them was fully aware that one was needed. As a couple, they didn't have a template for how to repair an old misstep. If he'd been able to understand how distressed Lisa was years ago, Philip might not have shut down her attempts to ask him about her concerns when they first came up. If he hadn't defensively rejected her questioning on their honeymoon, he could have told her then that he was sorry he didn't listen to her upset feelings on their wedding day and that nothing worrisome had happened the night before. She probably would have let it go. But, instead, the pain remained, although it stayed hidden, under the skin—like an abscess. By the time they arrived in my office, it had affected nearly everything in their relationship.

APOLOGIES HELP RELATIONSHIPS

One of the most pernicious myths about saying "I'm sorry" is that good relationships of any type or scale do not require apologies. Proponents of this myth believe that if you're in a good relationship, your mistakes, misunderstandings, and disagreements do not cause any harm. If you do hurt each other, you should somehow just understand the other person's intentions and move on. It isn't necessary to "go over the past."

On the contrary, the more important the relationship, the more crucial making a good apology can be, and the greater the cost of failing to employ one. Love does *not* mean never having to say you're sorry; love requires you to learn how to say you're sorry *well*.

In my experience, injuries that are not repaired or are inadequately addressed can erode the basis for a relationship. They rarely disappear fully. For example, one of the most common costs of an un-repaired injury shows up in repetitive patterns like the ones we saw with Philip and Lisa: The hurt settles into the fabric of the unfolding relationship, so that its overall pattern comes to resemble the original, unrepaired (sometimes forgotten) injury.

Here's one way it can happen: Lisa feels hurt by Philip and they don't resolve the problem together—or even talk about it. Her hurt goes underground and, without her thinking about it, colors how any future hurt by him—even a small thing—affects her. Any time he is thoughtless, it confirms and builds on how she felt before, bringing back a sad, familiar feeling. To her, he isn't just inattentively leaving her out of the picture hanging, for example; he is repeating and rein-forcing a hurtful pattern of excluding her. The shadow of unresolved hurt makes her see ambiguous behavior in the same light as his ear-lier actions, so she doesn't feel like cutting him a normal amount of slack. Thus, the disagreement over picture hanging plays on her orig-inal fear that she was left out of something important and worrisome before their wedding. She may tell her friend that he's become such a distant—or controlling or self-absorbed—guy that she doesn't rec-ognize him anymore. It can be completely outside of their conscious awareness, but this pattern re-creates her loneliness from the first hurt.

Initially, Philip is likely to be baffled and to react defensively to complaints he sees as groundless or at least overstated. The immediate triggers are indeed often arguable, which leads, predictably, to argu-ments. Responding to their own internal stories about what's going on leads to immensely frustrating conversations and more distance. Not until the original hurt is addressed satisfactorily do they have a chance for a fresh slate.

"I'm sorry" is number six on *HuffPost*'s "11 Things the Happiest Couples Say to Each Other All the Time."[1] The ability to deliver a sincere apology to your partner can make the difference between a small disagreement and a long-standing conflict. If a good repair isn't made, hurt between people can fester and build. Relationships like Lisa and Philip's can be lost. The earlier failure to fix their problem interfered with emotional intimacy and trust and led to lower "relationship esteem," that is, how they felt about their partnership itself. The bitterness they experienced was at risk of souring the good memories they still held.

Many couples have unproductive disagreements that are repeated for so long they become familiar scripts. If asked, they can usually quote "the fight we always have." Over time, such arguments become automatic, like the "muscle memory" of actions you can do with your eyes closed. Unfortunately, unthinking routines keep you from noticing what the other person actually means or feels in a given conversation; you can't see who they are in any particular moment if your eyes are closed. Alongside the rote arguments with a person you sincerely used to value—and still could if you were paying attention— grows loneliness.

In order to prevent some of this long-term squabbling, couples therapist and author Daphne de Marneffe recommends that couples learn how to fight during their engagements. As much a part of wedding planning as the guest list, they "should also think about how they will cope with disagreement." You can practice managing conflict by addressing smaller, current problems with honesty and careful listening. The skills involved are not more complicated than a wedding reception seating chart, but much more crucial for a couple to develop.[2]

When you practice resolving hurt and misunderstanding, you can begin to unwind and unlearn your problematic patterns as a couple. It's like a shared fitness regimen: You become stronger at addressing hard moments as you get in "better shape." Like Philip and Lisa ultimately did, you also can rediscover what you value about each other and establish ways to protect against getting stuck in such an unfortunate habitual routine again. Not only do you feel and function better, you're more confident about future challenges.

Of course, it's not only intimate couples who can suffer from lingering or festering hurt. Family members and friends often fail to find a way to face pain together. Unresolved hurt and unaddressed misunderstandings can lead to the loss of many important family connections and leave people isolated. However, almost any harm or breach, faced together with open minds and hearts, not only can be survived but can lead to a better relationship as well. Both the giver and the recipient of an effective apology feel better—about themselves, each other, and their connection. It's almost always a win-win proposition.

MAKING APOLOGIES HELPS YOU, TOO

My office can feel like a secular confessional, a forum for speaking things that need to be said and can't be said anywhere else. Many people seek therapy because of injuries they've sustained, but many also come in carrying regrets or the burden of harm they've caused to someone else. A widow needs to come to terms with having been unfaithful to her husband twenty-five years earlier. A man feels conflicted about his success because he cheated on a critical licensing exam. A woman is haunted by shady practices her boss pressured her to carry out. They want to make things right with others or with themselves, or both.

The thing is, not only does everyone make mistakes; practically everyone commits actual wrongdoing of one sort or another, too. We look at other people's missteps and see patterns of overtly bad behavior, cruelty, lawbreaking, wanton disregard for people, and so on, from which we can easily distance ourselves. (Whew, you may think, she's not talking about me!) But it can also be the error in judgment, the uncharacteristically slipshod performance, the overreaction that turns mean, the white lie that becomes a habit, the hidden mistake, the small cheat. Nearly everyone has been guilty of causing harm or pain to others, whether deliberately or accidentally. Simply put, we don't always live up to our wish for how we want to see ourselves in the world.

In some instances, you know when you've erred—even if you aren't willing to admit it. When you fail to follow your moral compass, when your arrows land wide of the mark, you feel it. In fact, this missing of the intended target is actually the original meaning of both the Greek and Hebrew words for "sin."[3]

I've met many people who have been unable to address their regrets, stymied for years by cultural myths or habits of thinking, stuck without a map toward making amends. Guilt can be helpful when it informs you that something needs to be fixed. But when you don't make something right, guilt accumulates, like silt in a river's waters that ends up lining the banks. Leftover guilt can thicken into self-condemnation and distort your sense of yourself. If you haven't been able to deal with something that you feel guilty about or if you've been forgiven too easily, you might find yourself avoiding the other person or distancing yourself from similar situations. You might become locked in repetitive conflicts in which you end up arguing your innocence, or stuck in a victim or aggressor role you don't want.

Some current cultural voices and popular media suggest that you should accept yourself just as you are, that you should simply forgive yourself, rather than feel regret for your mistakes. I argue that this "forgiveness inflation" causes not only relationship problems, but problems within the individual as well.

Gordon Marino, a professor of philosophy, wrote in the *New York Times* that "we can learn to let things go, but before we let them go, we have to let regret get hold of us."[4] For a person of conscience to feel better after regrettable actions, some form of repair or atonement is necessary. That is, until you somehow "fix" it, you carry the weight of what you've done wrong.

Why Apologize?

When we talk about a burden of guilt, the expressions we use overlap with spiritual language. We tend to regard wrongdoing as akin to sin, at least in the sense of our arrows flying wide of their marks. Regardless of whether or not mistakes are officially wrong, they seem to highlight a gap between our actions and our higher selves (or what some might think of as God). It is in this space that the painful regrets and moral quandaries I'm talking about in this book reside. When we don't make wrongs right, we suffer.

In contrast, when we do face ourselves and our actions, psychotherapist and writer Avi Klein says that relief, honor, and a sense of purpose follow. He has found that he has to help his clients face their true, negative feelings about themselves regarding regrettable behavior. Only then does growth occur. If people avoid dealing directly with the harm they've caused, they don't get better.[5]

When you are able to make amends for hurt in a relationship, you get to grow as a person. An accurate view of your responsibility can hurt, but it also expands your sense of yourself and enhances your personal and spiritual development. Outside of religious contexts, most of us don't talk much about the value of repentance or atonement. Secular approaches to personal development tend to treat guilt like a corrosive emotion, rather than a valuable impetus to fix something broken.

In much of Western culture, including politics and personal relationships, people just don't know how powerful and important it is to face their wrongdoing—whether with other people or a higher power. Even beloved writer Anne Lamott describes in a book title what she regards as the most important prayers: *Help, Thanks, Wow: The Three Essential Prayers*. But I think she left out another important one: *Sorry*.[6]

Even when a relationship is over, it may be worth trying to fix something you regret.

Diana behaved very badly when Tommy, her boyfriend of many

years, broke up with her after college. My sense is that he behaved badly, too, but she went further than he did. She created fake social media accounts and cyberstalked his new girlfriend. Using highly personal information about him, she posted false, incriminating stories. She persisted until her anger burned out, more than a year later.

In the following years, she dated other people but couldn't shake the specter of what had happened with Tommy. At first, she thought she couldn't get close to someone new because of the way he broke up with her, but finally she realized that she didn't trust *herself*. She'd acted with such hostility that she had trouble coming to terms with it.

Approaching thirty, she'd been in therapy for a year or so when she heard that Tommy's beloved uncle had died. She wrote him a sympathy letter saying that she was sorry about the loss of Uncle Antony. (That's the condolence version of "I'm sorry.") She went on to an apology: "I'm also sorry about how I acted after we broke up. I really regret what I did and the hurt I probably caused you. I hope you're doing well—aside from your grief, of course."

He responded graciously: "It wasn't either of our finest hours. Thank you for your sympathy about losing Antony." For years Diana had carried a sense of guilt and responsibility for her hostile stalking. After their communication, despite their relationship being long over, she felt lighter about the repair they made.

Just as there is no statute of limitations on hurt, there's also no time limit on feeling bad about having hurt someone. When the *New York Times* invited men to report their sexual misconduct from when they were in high school, hundreds of people wrote about events that still troubled them several decades later.[7] Similarly, thirty years after hitting a parked car and leaving the scene, an anonymous offender sent a thousand dollars to the South St. Paul, Minnesota, police department. The sender asked them to pass it on to the car's owner, if possible, expressed remorse, and asked for forgiveness. Chief Bill

Messerich guessed that the offense was "weighing on this person's conscience [and] they wanted to try to make things right."[8]

Unresolved hurts can eat at you, limit you in ways that don't seem to make sense, and wake you in the middle of the night. The proper reckoning with harmful mistakes makes an enormous difference in your life. To be sure, it's not easy to do, but it seems downright wasteful not to try.

YOU NEED PEOPLE

If you don't repair rifts between you and another person, the most wasteful outcome is that you lose the relationship. Aside from the specific people you'd hate to lose, you need people in your life for more reasons than you might think. You're probably aware of the emotionally painful loneliness that can accompany loss and isolation. In addition, though, we are also learning more about the profound costs to your physical health. For the past several decades, many psychologists have studied the important role social connections play in people's health. A 2010 review of research studies showed that lacking social relationships has an influence on the risk of death that's comparable to smoking and alcohol consumption.[9]

This has been such a huge area of research that the American Psychological Association published two special issues of journals presenting research findings that illustrate the many ways close relationships favorably affect your health.[10] These robust research findings underscore the concern raised by the "loneliness epidemic" identified by Surgeon General Vivek Murthy in 2018.[11]

I certainly don't claim that all social isolation or lack of relationships is caused by a failure to make effective repairs. What I do find, though, is that unresolved conflicts can lead to chronic dissatisfaction and consequent distance or estrangement.

A Good Apology

SAME STORY, LARGER STAGE

In 2013, Israeli prime minister Benjamin Netanyahu made an unexpected telephone call to his Turkish counterpart, Recep Tayyip Erdoğan, to issue a personal apology. Three years earlier, an Israeli raid against an aid flotilla had killed nine Turkish civilians, leading to very strained relations between the two countries. The three-year deadlock had included restrictions on Israeli training flights and interrupted diplomatic relations. Mr. Erdoğan had been quoted as making critical comments about Zionism. Near the end of a prolonged meeting with President Barack Obama, Mr. Netanyahu called Mr. Erdoğan and expressed his regret for the errors that led to the loss of lives and deterioration of the nations' ties. He also committed to a compensation plan that would provide restitution for those who died. After the conversation, both leaders emphasized the historical importance of the centuries-long international friendship and strong cooperation.

If Mr. Netanyahu hadn't changed his previous position, the connection between the two countries would probably have deteriorated further. Instead, their relations were greatly improved by his apology.[12] He didn't change the past harm done to the Turkish people, of course, but he made a different future possible.

Leaders have the power to make things different, to help heal past harms. When I witness the positive power of an effective apology, it makes me long to see them elsewhere, in other situations involving harm, misunderstandings, and blocked potential for a better future.

But a missed public apology or an incomplete one keeps pain alive and prevents healing. A confusing apology made to "Native Peoples" began as a US Senate resolution in 2009. It was worded in legalese and contained many statements that began with the word "whereas."[13] By the time President Obama signed a watered-down version, it had been embedded in a Department of Defense appropriations act. Although the apology was still historic, it was not highlighted.

Many people, including Native Americans, have never heard about it.[14] This ineffective and unsatisfying apology caused much puzzlement and pain, including for Layli Long Soldier, an enrolled member of the Oglala Sioux Tribe. In her book of poetry called *Whereas*, she poignantly wrestles with what the government failed to say. She writes of learning to exist "without the slightest conjunctions to connect me. Without an exchange of questions, without the courtesy of answers. It is mine, this unholding."[15]

This apology didn't involve the people who were putatively addressed and it didn't go as far as it could have. It didn't heal historic injuries much, if at all.

John Kador, who writes about best practices in leadership, describes how, frequently, "a well-spoken apology defused resentment, created good will, and, more times than not, mysteriously transformed a relationship ruptured by mistrust and disappointment into something stronger and more durable than it was before."[16] Mr. Kador views an apology not as a sign of weakness, but as a signal of strength, transparency, and accountability. As in personal relationships, an apology in the workplace "is the practice of extending ourselves because we value the relationship more than we value the need to be right."[17] Apologizing is a leadership skill that is critical for our time. It is, he says, "humanity's perfect response to imperfection."[18]

In the public marketplace, if companies fail to address the complaints of their customers or clients with goodwill and responsiveness, their reputations can suffer—which leads to diminished success. Direct acknowledgment and apology are well documented to be effective: Those customers whose complaints were resolved satisfactorily become 30 percent more loyal than those who never complained.[19] Furthermore, research from Boston University's business school shows that customers prefer businesses that corrected a mistake over ones that hadn't made a mistake at all.[20] This makes sense in the same way that you can trust a relationship more if you've successfully faced a problem.

Within work groups, facing and handling intrateam conflicts is what leads to the growth of trust, as well as greater accountability and commitment to the team's goals. Business leaders should help their teams approach disagreements, including emotional conflict, as opportunities rather than problems to be avoided.[21] Indeed, business strategist Lisa Earle McLeod teaches that avoiding conflict can keep coworkers trapped in it forever. As in personal relationships, a disagreement, misunderstanding, or interpersonal offense doesn't go away unless it's dealt with.[22]

Approaching intrateam functioning from a different angle, Harvard Business School professor Amy Edmondson was curious about whether better hospital work teams actually made fewer mistakes than others. What she found surprised her: The most cohesive teams reported more mistakes, not fewer. However, it turned out that they didn't actually make more; instead, they were more able and willing to talk about them. She adopted the term "psychological safety" to describe the type of team in which people raise questions and tell the truth about errors. She and others have found this factor strongly linked to successful performance in many ventures, including businesses.[23] In a recent interview, she suggested that the term "psychological safety" could give the wrong impression. She's not talking about "coziness"; she's talking about "candor."[24] A workplace can foster psychological safety by focusing on potential solutions to problems, rather than on determining who's to blame for them. I would call this encouragement to face mistakes and failures crucial advice not only for workplace groups, but also for successful relationships everywhere. You can't fix mistakes if you can't acknowledge them. As James Baldwin wrote, "Not everything that is faced can be changed, but nothing can be changed until it is faced."[25]

Why Apologize?

* * *

A basic distinction arises in these stories. Our resistance to admitting error and our failure to apologize well lead to continued hurt and conflict. In contrast, when we face our regrets thoroughly, we see profound, even transformational effects in many contexts and at any scale.

CHANGING THE STORY

No one wants to be blamed for something going wrong. Most of us are inclined to shy away from accepting fault. The urge to argue or protect your point makes sense if the goal is to be right or blameless. But going to the mat insisting on your rightness works in the wrong direction in most human engagements. In relationships, this kind of battle can be won only by losing; that is, you may be right, but you won't be closely connected. You won't end up feeling like you're on the same team. You won't understand each other better.

According to a report in the *Harvard Business Review* by Judith Glaser, author and business consultant, "your brain is hooked on being right." She describes the reinforcing power of the adrenaline that bathes your brain during a competitive argument. But, interestingly, she also reports that oxytocin, the hormone activated by our attachment to another person, feels comparably pleasurable. Not only that, it opens up networks in the prefrontal cortex, which further increases our ability to trust.[26] Psychologists have further found that oxytocin, alongside actual social support, directly dampens the harmful effects of stress on a person's body.[27] Even from a physiological standpoint, connection can be a better choice than being right.

All of this is to say that we are wired to benefit (personally, socially, and physically) from connections with other people. It follows that it can be of crucial importance to restore these ties after breaches or harms. Between any two people, the same issues hold, whether they're coworkers or a doctor and her patient.

Traditionally, in American medicine, a clinician who caused an injury adopted a deny-and-defend stance. The result was that the hurt patient and family were left with no information about what had gone wrong and no help to process a harmful, sometimes lethal outcome. The doctor was presumed to be correct, and, as a result, these patients often felt "guilty, afraid, and alone," as a column in the *New England Journal of Medicine* described it. Often the doctor felt guilty and isolated as well. No one knew how to talk about these errors, much less heal some of the harm done.[28]

Without an apology, "a patient's desire for comfort and understanding [becomes] a need for vengeance."[29] Rather than facing the error together and reaching a resolution that promotes the patient's recovery, "silence and evasion breed mistrust."[30] Malpractice suits result. This system costs everyone—unnecessarily.

In 2001, the University of Michigan Health System, led by attorney and clinical safety director Richard Boothman, began an ambitious shift toward a more responsible and personal process. Since then, they have provided full disclosure of medical errors to patients and, when appropriate, apologies and offers of compensation. It's ironic that one of the biggest roadblocks to physicians' taking responsibility for their medical errors has been the fear of litigation; in 2010, the Michigan system reported that their rates of lawsuits went down, as did their costs for liability and patient compensation. In addition, the time between the report of an injury and its resolution also declined, which benefited patients and families.[31]

One patient, Jennifer Wagner, was incorrectly reassured about a breast lump that later turned out to be advanced breast cancer. She required a complete mastectomy, chemotherapy, and radiation. She was understandably plagued by worry about her young children. As she and her lawyer prepared for a lawsuit, Mr. Boothman's system asked five impartial doctors to review her records. They concluded that her physician had indeed erred. In an "earnest" two-hour meeting between Ms. Wagner and her doctors at the University of Michigan, they discussed in detail what had gone wrong and the medical team explained her current medical status and prognosis. Afterward, she said, "I felt like I had finally been heard. I can't even describe how euphoric I felt when I left that meeting." Over time, her fatigue improved, she returned to work, and she received four hundred thousand dollars for her sons' college funds. This outcome was less expensive for the hospital than a lengthy malpractice trial would have been and moreover was more humane for Ms. Wagner.[32] She received not only a financial acknowledgment of the error, but also an emotional one.

Doing the right thing is what we're talking about here, but it doesn't always seem clear what that is. Rather than speaking directly to tragic errors and seeking to promote healing, people sometimes try to protect their own. In contrast, sometimes a quick, responsible reaction to a harmful mistake prevents a more serious negative outcome. In 2018, in the highly charged national context of deadly police encounters with black citizens, Boston Police Department (BPD) officers were called to deal with two African American boys playing with a toy gun, a realistic replica. A black bystander, "Brother Lawrence" Dugan, filmed the police response. A BPD sergeant, Henry Staines, became angry and confronted Mr. Dugan about the filming and shoved the replica weapon toward the citizen. The heated confrontation itself was filmed and posted online. It generated understandable, predictable outrage.

What wasn't predictable was the strong, immediate response by then commissioner William Evans, who said he was sorry on behalf of his department and clarified that citizens do indeed have the right to record police actions. His apology was followed by an extensive expression of remorse by Sergeant Staines. The quick, thorough, and apparently sincere apologies by the BPD were credited with "transforming what could have been an embittering episode of police intimidations into a reassuring demonstration of police accountability."[33]

In this public case, thorough and genuine statements went a long way toward addressing at least some of the immediate harm done. The police apologies didn't solve the larger, systemic problems that still afflict the communities involved, but they changed the immediate conversation. Badly handled, this kind of situation could have exploded into more damage. Lives could have been lost if the BPD had chosen to assert its "rightness" over its responsibility to heal the harm it caused. My hope is that a good apology puts out the immediate-harm spark and lets the more important conversations continue.

In Boston, for example, important changes were already in the works and continued after this event: The BPD expanded its program to outfit its police officers with body cameras, and District Attorney Rachael Rollins—the first female person of color in the position—was elected, partially on a platform of reducing police violence and incarceration.[34] Furthermore, in 2018, Massachusetts passed a sweeping criminal justice reform bill aiming to decrease incarceration rates.[35] Potentially positive steps like these could be overshadowed by a heat-of-the-moment mistake *and, especially, the failure to repair it.*

In a much less weighty but more widely witnessed exchange, *Saturday Night Live* comedian Pete Davidson made tasteless jokes about a Republican congressional candidate who had lost his eye during Navy SEAL service in Afghanistan. Davidson's comment about Dan Crenshaw's eye patch, "I know he lost his eye in war—or whatever," netted a universally negative reaction, which led to an invitation for Mr. Crenshaw to appear on the show. First, Mr. Davidson stated his regret "from the bottom of my heart," saying that "the man is a war hero and deserves all the respect in the world." He then acknowledged that "if any good came of this maybe it was that for one day, the left and the right finally came together to agree on something. That I'm a dick."

His guest used the opportunity to underscore that the political left and right can indeed agree on some things. Mr. Crenshaw demonstrated how we can forgive one another and see the good in one another, even after hurtful actions. In this case, it wasn't only the apology itself, but also the effective use made of it by its recipient, that was so constructive.[36]

The stories in this chapter reveal both that failures to make apologies can be very costly and that efforts toward repair and rebuilding trust can contribute not only to individuals and to personal relationships, but also to an organization's and even a nation's recovery from harm.

This humble process has enormous personal, spiritual, and relationship payoffs. So, why is it so hard?

BENEFITS OF GOOD APOLOGIES

In relationships

- **Healing from hurt**
- **More positive feelings, greater closeness between people**
- **Higher "relationship esteem"**
- **Increased confidence about facing the next conflict**
- **Enlarged future possibilities**
- **Retaining relationships**

For yourself

- **Personal and spiritual value of taking responsibility and addressing guilt**
- **More oxytocin in your system**
- **More social connections, leading to positive health outcomes**

In medicine

- **Greater satisfaction for patients and families**
- **Better possibility of healing for all parties**
- **Potential for decrease in malpractice suits**

In business settings

- **Greater trust in organizations that handle mistakes well**
- **More "psychological safety" in workplaces**
- **Increased commitment, trust, and creativity on work teams**

In the larger community

- **Reduced tension and conflict between larger groups**
- **Better possibility of healing from historical injustices**
- **Better community relations with the police**

CHAPTER 2

It's So Very Hard to Do

Rolland, a forty-three-year-old attorney, came to see me at the recommendation of his girlfriend, Cathy. During our meetings, he spoke relatively freely about his romantic relationship, his social life, and his work. With humor and insight, he told stories about his childhood, especially involving his only sibling, a just-younger brother. Both Rolland's parents had died in the previous five years, and the dark periods of grief he experienced were why Cathy thought he should talk to someone.

As he spoke about his parents, particularly his mother, his voice slowed and sometimes his eyes filled. But he usually moved quickly on to another subject. As a litigator, Rolland was used to controlling the narrative. In response to an unexpected question from me, he often complimented me on my "good question," but his considerable verbal skills enabled him to skirt direct answers. He didn't avoid all unhappy, complicated material: He told me that conflicts with Cathy could be heated—as could those with colleagues. He labeled himself "kind of a hard-ass" and was receptive to considering that his temper sometimes caused him trouble.

When I inquired about trusted friends, Rolland responded that Cathy was the only person he was close to—anymore. The "anymore" rang hollow and sad, as if he was alluding to a lost confidant.

"Did you have someone else before?"

"No! Well, I don't know." He became uncharacteristically quiet. I waited.

After a moment, he began a courtroom anecdote I'd heard before, well-worn, with a funny punch line.

When he paused, midstory, I gently interjected, "Was it your mother? The person you used to be close to?"

"What? No!"

His eyes narrowed and he rearranged himself in his chair, rolling his neck. "She wasn't that kind of mother."

Silence, except for his breath, which came in audible, short bursts. I wondered if I'd angered him by interrupting his story, but his eyes looked more bereft than angry. Feelings ran across his face like racing clouds on a sunny day.

Finally, he sighed, dropped his shoulders, and looked directly at me. His voice was tight with hard feeling, barely making it through his teeth.

"My asshole brother and I used to be close."

Rolland told me that, five years earlier, just after their father died, his brother and he had argued about their parents' property. On one occasion, they'd come to blows, which started when Rolland pushed his brother in frustration. In the melee that followed, his brother had broken Rolland's nose and then stormed out of the house, leaving him bloody and furious. They hadn't spoken since.

His brother, who had been his close ally in childhood stories, disappeared from his life.

"He didn't even speak to me at our mother's funeral." His jaw tightened and he shook his head. "That ruined our relationship for good."

Over the next few sessions, we explored their conflict. Carefully, I introduced the possibility that Rolland had inadvertently contributed to the standoff. For example, he hadn't approached his brother at the funeral, either.

"No, *he* betrayed *me!*"

Eventually, he went so far as to say, "He owes me an apology. I wish he would say he was sorry."

Despite the loss of this important relationship, Rolland couldn't consider approaching his brother to try to repair their rift. I don't mean to imply that Rolland's brother was blameless, only that Rolland played a role, too. But he could not imagine apologizing for his part.

You could see Rolland's isolation as self-imposed, a result of his innate stubbornness, but I see it as a product of our culture, too. In a recent *Psychology Today* report, a journalist interviewed estranged siblings. Despite years of unhappy distance, they *all* said they would be willing to reconcile if their brother or sister approached them to say "I'm sorry." But *not one* intended to initiate an apology.[1] A collaborative study between the Centre for Family Research at the University of Cambridge and the nonprofit Stand Alone reported that breaks between family members always carry a steep price, even when they're also accompanied by feelings of relief.[2]

So, why do we, like Rolland—like all these estranged siblings—stay stuck in unhappy situations rather than fix them?

In my experience, mending these breaches seems incredibly hard to do, usually for both parties. Most of us rarely consider apologizing when a rift has occurred. You may sense you've played a part, but it's especially hard to apologize when you've been hurt yourself. Deep down, you might believe that there's more than one side to the story, but you still stay stuck. Rolland wasn't able to consider the other side, at least not during the time I knew him.

Most of us have a Rolland in our lives—or are like Rolland ourselves. If you have trouble taking responsibility for mistakes or hurts or conflicts that have more than one side, you are not alone. Because of the way our brains work, we are biased to have hardwired limitations in the awareness of our errors. Further, loads of societal rules and cultural norms operate directly against our being able to make amends. In the West, particularly in the United States, our dominant culture values a posture of rightness and certainty, which doesn't lend itself to paying attention to how we might have hurt someone. Because our models of psychological strength lean toward competitiveness and independence, relationship repair barely makes a blip on our radar.

We also have sparse models and receive almost no instruction about how to make mistakes or wrongs right. We're fascinated by the attempts of politicians or entertainers to get out of trouble, but most of the public apologies we hear about are inadequate and sometimes downright awful. Although we can all probably relate to the wish to hide from disapproval, our eagle-eyed inner critics can identify the ways these amends fail to make things right. Unfortunately, we're not likely to witness many personal apologies, whether effective or not. Confusing the picture further are some common uses of the words "I'm sorry" that we can mistake for actual apologies, when they have different meanings. Naturally, it follows that most of us don't know what a really good, thorough apology looks like.

Given all these limitations, it's kind of amazing that anyone ever apologizes in a meaningful way. Whether because it's easier or simply familiar, many of us accept the sad conclusion that once something's gone badly, that's the end of the story. But you wouldn't be reading this book if you were satisfied by that state of affairs. I wouldn't have written it if I believed we were doomed to that fate.

So let's talk about why a simple apology is so challenging. First we'll look at neuroscientific limitations, then we'll move on to aspects of current culture that contribute to the difficulty of apologizing, and finally we'll discuss the dearth of good models.

COGNITIVE AND PERCEPTUAL BIASES

Some of the challenge in making a good apology stems from the way our brains work. On a biological level, our perceptual equipment is geared toward simplicity. From the beginning, human infants can see only eight to fifteen inches away from their eyes and only high-contrast shapes. We begin life able to perceive only our own very small world and only in black-and-white clarity.

It's easy to imagine how that type of physical brain function contributes to our ways of thinking. As children, we begin with a limited, all-or-none, here-or-gone perspective. As soon as toddlers develop object permanence—the ability to remember that something exists even though they can't see it anymore—the situation begins to get more complicated. That is, things can be *both* here and gone.

Moral understanding similarly grows from absolute right versus wrong to more complexity (and more relatedness) as we mature. Carol Gilligan's description of an ethic of care, mentioned in the introduction, teaches us that how our behavior affects another person can be a crucial lens through which to view morality. Considering another person's point of view or inviting a more complex understanding of events requires acceptance of in-between, gray tones.

Under conditions of stress or threat, though, we can all return to narrow, yes-or-no thinking. Life seems clearer if we settle on a basic matrix, such as "Someone's right and someone's wrong...and I'm the one who's right."

If the stress is extreme, we are reduced to the fight-flight-freeze options you've heard about. These reactions are driven by the limbic system, not the cortical, cerebral regions of the brain. You might say we don't think; we just react.

But, even under the best of circumstances, our senses are routinely subject to a surprising degree of distortion. Our perception—the way our brains decipher sensory information—and cognition—the way we think—follow suit. That includes outright fabrication and misremembering. In her delightful exploration of "wrongology," journalist Kathryn Schulz presents a mountain of evidence that speaks to how and why humans are so prone to error. We "see" and "know" things that are just plain inaccurate. Ms. Schulz examines optical illusions that our eyes fall for, even when our thinking brains are aware that we're being deceived. One example is the visual phenomenon known as the arctic mirage, a peculiar bending of light near the earth's poles. In 1818 this phenomenon convinced Scottish explorer John Ross that distant mountains were actually near his location in Baffin Bay. The illusion led him to miss the Northwest Passage entirely, a mistake that crucially damaged his career.[3] Lest we think these occasions are anomalous, Ms. Schulz reminds us of the mistaken view that celestial bodies revolve around the earth, a "truth" that held sway for centuries. The "reality" of the flat earth was apparent to everyone for a very long time.

In theory, we'd all agree that everybody makes mistakes. But, in the heat of a moment, we rarely believe that applies to us, or to the present situation, or under these particular conditions. This inability to see our own mistakes appears to be a genuine, brain-based limitation in our perception. Most telling in Ms. Schulz's report is the extent to which people believe they are right, even when errors are evident.

In general, we're all probably wrong a lot more often than we think. We are biased to see other people's mistakes and remain blind to our own. As Ms. Schulz observes, "Most of our indiscriminate enjoyment of being right is matched by an almost equally indiscriminate feeling that we *are* right."[4] Remember consultant Judith Glaser, who went so far as to say that we are addicted to being right, drawn to the adrenaline rushes that accompany debate?[5]

I want to be sure to make it plain here: *Error blindness is not mere willfulness. It is our wiring.* This strong, innate tendency in all of us illustrates what we're up against when we try to take responsibility for our mistakes in the world.

None of this is to say that it can't be overruled.

Confirmation bias. Beyond the inevitability of both our making mistakes and our blindness to them, specific cognitive patterns create additional problems for us. The first of these is confirmation bias, the overwhelming tendency to give more weight to evidence that confirms our beliefs than to evidence that challenges them. For example, this is how the Salem witch trials found evidence for witchcraft, regardless of the outcome of their tests. In one such examination, mistakes while reciting the Lord's Prayer were believed to indicate that the speaker was a witch. But accused sorcerer George Burroughs's perfect recitation was labeled a "devil's trick" and he was hanged anyway.[6] We seek out and pay attention to information that matches what we already know, and we both fail to seek out counterevidence and ignore it if we do find it.

Challenging this thinking pattern isn't impossible, as we'll see in Chapter 3, but it does require a deliberate change of habit.

Selective inattention, also called "inattentional blindness," can also cause perceptual and cognitive errors. We're looking at one thing or in one direction and miss information that would be completely evident if we looked in a different direction. This is the way magicians and street thieves cause you to focus on one thing (an endless flowing scarf or a confederate asking for directions) while other, more crucial action takes place (the card goes up the sleeve or your pocket gets picked).

A series of studies asked participants to watch a short video of people passing basketballs back and forth. In various conditions, subjects were instructed to count the passes or otherwise focus on what was going on among the people on-screen. Between one-third and one-half of all viewers did not see a person wearing a gorilla suit enter the scene and beat on his chest before exiting—presumably because they were focused on something else. The gorilla didn't fit the way viewers' brains organized the action in the video.[7] As the study became well-known and subsequent viewers learned about the gorilla in advance, people were more likely to look for and see the gorilla in a modified clip, but they missed other unanticipated events.[8]

A related study looked at whether radiologists might be subject to inattentional blindness as they searched for lung nodules on CT scans. What researchers at Brigham and Women's Hospital in Boston found was that twenty of twenty-four experts failed to see an image of a gorilla added to lung films, a white-outlined figure that was forty-eight times the size of the average nodule they did find! When prompted, 100 percent of the radiologists could easily see and identify the image they'd missed earlier.[9] Perhaps it's reassuring to you that well-trained, completely competent radiologists have the same kind of blind spot the rest of us have. Looked at another way, it could be disturbing that we all have this kind of limitation.

In a relationship, as between Rolland and his brother, your attention might be "selectively" focused on your own hurt, that is, on how the other person did you wrong. Selective inattention makes you genuinely less likely to notice any ways you might have hurt the other person.

You may have picked up this book for your partner, hoping, like Rolland and many estranged family members, that someone else would apologize to you. It's not a bad idea, to learn how to get the apology you are longing for, the amends you need from someone in order to have the relationship you want. But I also want to challenge you to think of an apology process as a two-sided construction effort: Let's say you're on one side of a painful chasm of disagreement and your partner (or friend or family member) is on the far side. What the two of you need is a bridge that can span your differences. Above dangerous waters, trust and mutuality may be your best tools for a project that ultimately succeeds. If you want to build a structure that can connect the two sides, it will help to pay attention to those shadowy, less obvious contributions you might have made to the troubling space between you. But as you will see, our natural inclinations can keep us forever on opposite sides, sure that we're right.

Cognitive dissonance. In the mid-twentieth century, psychologist Leon Festinger and his colleagues identified another thinking problem, called cognitive dissonance. His term describes the difficulty our brains have when confronted with conflicting or contradictory information, a phenomenon that has yielded a massive body of social psychological research. Dr. Festinger's first, famous finding concerned the followers of a doomsday prophet they referred to as Marian Keech, who was certain that the world would end on December 21, 1954. At midnight the faithful were to gather together so they could be ushered to safety aboard a spaceship. When midnight passed, the devastated group sat in stunned silence, awaiting cataclysmic doom. After the next day dawned and dimmed as days normally do, the faithful did not, as you might expect, change or question their belief. They explained the apparent contradiction by concluding that their faithful watch in the night had "shed so much light" that God had canceled the end of the world. Prior to this doom that didn't come, they'd been reluctant to talk about their convictions, but afterward they began an enthusiastic campaign to spread the word. Instead of questioning their beliefs, the followers' faith became more fervent and certain.[10]

Cognitive dissonance refers to the discomfort you feel when you hold two contradictory ideas (the world would end and yet the world didn't end) or an idea and an action (drinking excessively is bad for you and yet here you are at the liquor store picking up a couple of bottles of Captain Morgan). In response to this discomfort, you may change your mind or your actions to resolve the contradiction, but that can be very hard to do, especially if you're invested in them, as the doomsday believers were. You will probably resolve the dissonance by convincing yourself that the false, discredited belief isn't false or the harmful behavior isn't harmful.

This isn't exactly a choice. Neuroscience has shown that the reasoning areas of the brain virtually shut down when you're confronted with this kind of dissonance, whereas the emotional circuits light up when consonance is restored.[11] In your brain, cognitive dissonance "longs" to be resolved and tends to do so along the easiest path possible.

If you believe (or want to believe) you're not the kind of person who causes harm, cognitive dissonance can interfere with seeing yourself as responsible for the hurt someone else feels. If it seems to you that someone else's actions are obviously hurtful to you and you can't understand why they won't acknowledge it, consider the likelihood that a similar dissonance exists in their mind. They could well be blocked from realizing they caused harm because that idea conflicts with others they hold. Most of us don't want to engage in a reckoning that may show us to be different than we think we are or may reveal our understanding of important things to be in error. That's one reason Rolland couldn't consider another perspective on what happened with his brother. He had a story and a belief about why their relationship broke apart—namely, that his brother had wrecked things—and he was sticking to it.

We hurt each other by mistake, unintentionally, all the time. But because that action contradicts other information we have—our intentions, our self-concept—it's hard to see, hard to consider, hard to believe.

Self-justification. Another dissonance-related brain phenomenon, self-justification, works similarly: We are biased to view our own actions as essentially legitimate, particularly in contrast to how we view others'. In a relationship, it can show up like this: When you argue or fight with your partner, you might believe that your behavior represents your inherent and valued qualities. Self-justification prevents you from asking, "Am I wrong? Could I be making a mistake?" When your partner disagrees with you, you make sense of the disagreement by seeing the other person's position as faulty or flawed. Then, by way of confirmation bias, you find more instances of their blameworthy ideas or actions. Basic cognitive dissonance prevents you from judging your own less-than-ideal behavior.[12] The relationship's decline begins to gain momentum.

When someone divorces because of actual abuse, they don't require any additional justification. But if you are torn about divorcing, dissonance theory predicts that you will resolve your mixed feelings by heightening your negative perceptions of your ex-spouse. Self-justification is the route by which ambivalence morphs into certainty and rage.

Linking all these cognitive and perceptual biases are two basic tendencies: You can't help but perceive the world from your own point of view, which can lead to misconceptions, and you are driven to continue thinking and doing what you have already thought and done. Change can be terribly challenging. To consider our unintended, unwitnessed, untoward effects on other people is, for many of us, brand-new. Taking on any new approach (such as learning to apologize) can add biological stresses to the already loaded brain. Because of evolutionary pressures, the brain's more "primitive" functions (those based in the limbic system or the amygdala) privilege both fear and anger over rational processes or thinking (located in the cortical regions). When people face uncertainty, strong feelings can swamp considered reasoning. As a result, there's always a risk that rising emotions can derail a more thoughtful repair process. By all that, I mean that you can lose your head and forget that your most important goal might be reconnection.

To learn any new skill involves some missteps and frustration. The unfamiliar terrain of making amends can lead to discouragement, doubt, and pessimism. It's no wonder Rolland didn't see a solution he could employ with his brother. People often don't.

But that doesn't mean it's impossible.

CULTURAL FACTORS

Like the air we breathe, cultural norms and expectations can be invisible. Although deeply embedded in each of us, they operate as unquestioned assumptions. We learn some of them through direct teaching and many more from observations throughout our lives, beginning very early, before we have language to capture our experience. From our families, neighbors, clergy, teachers, friends, and later coworkers and bosses, we learn how we're supposed to behave. Many social expectations in Western cultures influence us in a direction precisely opposite from making apologies.

Rolland, for example, grew up in a somewhat conventional home in a largely white, midwestern suburb. His father was a dominant patriarch who ruled his household, including his wife, with a stern, my-way-or-the-highway style. His boys were taught not to question rules and not to show vulnerability. As in many authoritarian systems, maleness itself—or a particular form of maleness—was valued; it was an insult to refer to anyone as a "girl" or other terms that imply femaleness (hence weakness). As boys, Rolland and his brother learned to work hard and to admire the superheroes of the day, like Superman and Batman, who rarely showed emotion. The family also valued physical prowess, and they both competed in sports. Rolland's many friendships were relatively superficial and didn't last much past his student days. Through his young adulthood, he found his primary emotional connections with a series of girlfriends—and, in the background, his brother.

Rolland grew up a success story, a smart and competitive kid who made his parents proud. They all shared the perspective that his academic and professional achievements were due to his individual strengths and effort, and as a result he became quite confident overall. He became a good litigator, he says, because he never doubted himself.

As cultural models go, Rolland ably stands in for one long-dominant image of a successful adult as someone who is independent and confident. This ideal person, the teaching goes, should always win and should believe in the rightness, indeed, righteousness, of his or her position. Action is valued over contemplation and especially over feelings. Any feelings other than anger are particularly difficult to access or accept—either in yourself or in others—because you are trying to avoid vulnerability and doubt. Understandably, from this perspective, you might view making an apology as a sign of weakness, as an option that's completely off the table.

Masculine model. Some of the cultural ideal we learn is tied to a particular model of manhood, the solitary hero who doesn't need anyone else. The American Psychological Association recently put forward guidelines for addressing "traditional masculinity," which they describe as marked by emotional stoicism, dominance, competitiveness, and aggression.[13] The fact that this model does not reflect the wide range of people in Western cultures doesn't diminish the power of the image. The Marlboro Man of the twentieth century, a white man by himself in the wild, often mustachioed and often on a horse, still represents to many people how men are supposed to be. The Marlboro Man doesn't seem very likely to apologize.

It can take great courage to demonstrate a different kind of leadership or masculinity. In his first months in office, President Obama's speeches around the world often took responsibility for US mistakes, including "sacrificing our values" regarding imprisonment at Guantanamo Bay. For this, he received both admiration and widespread condemnation. He was accused of displaying weakness in his "top ten apologies."[14] A 2012 book by Mitt Romney revealed the contrast between different models of strength: *No Apology: The Case for American Greatness*.[15]

At about the same time, a bumper sticker that read "Real Presidents Don't Apologize for Their Countries" went into circulation. It was a remarkable display of one side of widely discrepant views concerning what makes a strong leader. It also illustrates a problem our culture has with making repairs. At the time of writing this book, a similar, extreme model is represented by the US president, who characteristically doesn't admit mistakes and who eschews apologies. To be strong, some believe we are supposed to stand by our actions and our side's perspective as if they are right and the only right ones. No exceptions and no doubts.

In a survey of adults estranged from their families, women are more likely to be out of contact with family members, but estrangements involving men are more likely to last longer—or go on forever.[16] It may be harder for men, as it was for Rolland, to bring themselves to approach an estranged family member to reconcile.

In addition to pressure to be independent and free of self-doubt, it's widely documented that many men face a particular challenge with expressions of feeling. This probably begins, at least in part, with childhood socialization that leaves young men without practice addressing difficult emotions and experiences. Rosalind Wiseman, who writes about both adolescent boys and girls, says that girls have language to talk about the toxic messages they get from the culture, but boys don't.[17]

Again, this is not intended to suggest that it's impossible for men to apologize; it just may be harder.

Success model. A related cultural assumption holds that the success, failure, and value of our leaders, most of whom are white men, exist in an individualistic light. Aside from a formulaic assessment of sports teams, we rarely celebrate interdependence. If as a culture we don't value the centrality of connections with other people, we have little reason to care about preserving relationships, much less repairing them.

A related factor that interferes with making amends is our preference for quick solutions. We admire clear, certain fixes. When they are not at hand, we tend to be impatient and ready to discard both relationships and belongings. I wish I could count how many times I've heard the phrases "Get over it and move on," "What's done is done," and the more recent popular line "It is what it is." There seems to be little appetite for step-by-step, slow rebuilding of trust, for example, or for thinking in general, as opposed to instant knowing.

Understanding the effect you have on someone else, addressing your mistakes, and making things right all take time.

Relationship model. It follows from these cultural factors, as well as the perceptual equipment with which we operate, that our understanding of relationships is oversimplified, too. A fairy-tale "happily ever after" suggests that ongoing, true love is simple. In movies, the credits roll as the happy couple embraces, implying smooth sailing into the future. This false premise leads to many people's outright surprise that real relationships take tending and attention, not to mention that they require helping each other through disappointments and failings. It's no wonder we don't know how to approach, much less heal, the ways we hurt one another. When we view others' public failings, we tend to veer from hyperbolic condemnation to shallow pseudo-acceptance, as if we knew the truth about what happened and what it meant. Online comments sections often fill with extreme, polarized comments. People seem to "choose sides" quickly. These knee-jerk reactions to complicated, painful human dilemmas fail both the doer of the deed and the person the deed was done to. On top of that, television programs that feature outsized expressions of emotional pain, and reality shows in which phony relationships are "performed," distort our sense of human connections even further. Televised reconciliations can be heartwarming but are unconvincing. We rarely witness interpersonal problems mended realistically. All these factors make it hard to take genuine responsibility for hurt you yourself may have caused.

Conflict models. As you have no doubt noticed, these limitations extend to political discourse, which seems unlikely to promote learning from one another. We live in a time when it's easier to divide than to unify. Public debates and disagreements often have the rhythm and flavor of food fights rather than reasoned conversation. At the moment, louder, more extreme speech, tweets, and social media posts catch our attention, whereas quieter consideration of another's point of view grows ever more rare. In this context, an apology, a small repair between people, seems like a finger in the cracking dike of human dignity and respect.

Yet, for all of the extreme rhetoric we see online, a powerful impediment to good repairs is a widespread reluctance to address conflicts directly. In most spheres of our lives, we tend to avoid initiating difficult conversations. Despite public "big talk," we "let sleeping dogs lie" when it comes to actually addressing a painful dilemma face-to-face. Because we fear stirring up problems, hurting another person's feelings, or being seen as a troublemaker, we don't tackle problems that could be solved. Long ago, there may have been a survival value to avoiding in-group conflict, but its costs seem to have outweighed its benefits by far.

Influential management consultant and speaker Patrick Lencioni describes fear of conflict as one of the worst dysfunctions of a work team. Perhaps counterintuitively, Mr. Lencioni has found that it is an *absence* of conflict that interferes with the development of successful teams.[18] Members who can disagree productively reach stronger solutions to shared challenges. Despite the great value of effective management of workplace conflict, a recent Stanford University study found that many leaders did not feel competent in this regard. Among two hundred CEOs studied, 43 percent rated conflict management skills as their highest developmental need.[19] Facing difficult subjects appears to be as hard on work teams as it is in relationships between two people—and as valuable.

But if we are reluctant to raise challenging subjects with other people, we are exponentially more resistant to hearing difficult feedback about ourselves from them. For many reasons, we don't want to hear that we've been wrong—which is a shame, because critical feedback is necessary for improvement in most efforts. But in the right-or-wrong culture in which we currently live, critique can make you feel small, inept, like a loser. So if the potential subject of a conversation could be about a mistake you've made or a misstep you've taken, you've got extra reason to run in the opposite direction. Rolland, for example, couldn't even consider that he might have contributed to the altercation and distance between himself and his brother.

Finally, we live in a highly litigious climate. Colored by our adversarial legal system, every disagreement is a potential win-lose battle in which you should try to prove the other person wrong. You don't have to be an attorney to hold the view that admitting fault could get you sued. For criminal matters, adversarial contests may yield the fairest outcomes, but for family court, they tragically thwart the best resolutions. During very difficult life moments, we force people into opposing positions, even, for example, when they will be parenting children together as divorced partners. Our legal system pushes people into greater opposition, rather than encouraging better communication and potential peacemaking.

All these cultural and societal pressures leave little room for responsible, self-reflecting people to react with both compassion and accountability. What are we supposed to do with our mixed feelings about the unrepaired hurts in our lives, much less our own culpability and guilt?

LACK OF SKILLS

Making an effective apology, facing wrongdoing, and repairing damaged relationships are among the most humble, yet most courageous human behaviors. Their power is unparalleled. Considering how ubiquitous our mistakes are, we have remarkably sparse and poorly developed methods for addressing failings. It isn't our plentiful errors themselves that cause the most pain; our failure to fix them is what breaks hearts and relationships.

Yet, despite the importance of making amends, there is very little cultural emphasis, much less educational or family guidance, in this humble process. The arena of child-rearing is plenty complicated and provides ample opportunities for all of us to feel inadequate. That's why I make parenting suggestions in sympathy, not judgment—and certainly not because I personally handled things correctly.

When a child hurts someone else, say, another child, the conventional practice is to teach the child to mumble a rote, pro forma "I'm sorry," as if that's what is needed. Children learn to say words they don't understand and therefore don't mean. Rewarding these

42

words isn't the worst thing a parent can do, but saying "I'm sorry" before understanding the injury doesn't teach more important lessons about empathy or responsibility. The emphasis isn't on the other person's hurt or repairing the harm. Rarely is there an inquiry or a genuine statement of regret, much less restitution or prevention of future harm. Contrary to popular opinion about the two-word solution, saying "I'm sorry" is not the most important, or first, step in an effective apology; in fact, those exact words aren't actually necessary at all.

Also, we are commonly confused by two kinds of "I'm sorrys" that look like apologies but aren't. The "I'm sorry" that expresses sympathy, condolence, or caring about someone's suffering, as in "I'm sorry for your loss," is not an apology. When someone is hurt, we say, "I'm so sorry to hear about your accident [or illness]." We don't mean that we are remorseful, only that we feel empathy for the person. Any confusion that results is a drawback of the fact that the word "sorry" means more than one thing.

You probably know people who contribute to another source of confusion, the language overlap that results from saying the words "I'm sorry" all the time, for no particular reason. You might be one of those people. Women commonly joke among ourselves about how we make automatic apologies, even when someone else bumps into us, even to furniture. Some cultural observers suggest that this habit detracts from a woman's personal authority and power[20] and, particularly in professional negotiations, distracts from a woman's accomplishments.[21]

The hilarious handbook *How to Be a Canadian (Even If You Already Are One)* presents a program for mastering twelve different kinds of "I'm sorry," along with the characterization that Canadians use that expression the way cabdrivers use car horns, for just about any situation that comes along. The authors conclude that Canadians say "sorry" an awful lot. But they rarely make meaningful statements of regret.[22]

The reflexive habit decidedly isn't an apology and serves instead as a communication device rather than a repair attempt. Sometimes it interferes with a genuine apology. We can be so quick to go through the motions of remorse that we don't allow the time to experience it. We can mistake what has become a social habit or almost a verbal tic for real responsibility taking.

From the international leader to the neighbor, most of us don't really tackle interpersonal damage because we simply don't know how. During recent years, as public figures have dealt with their mistakes and wrongdoing, we've seen responses that range from defensive counteraccusations to opportunities that were missed entirely. For example, the high-profile men accused of sexual mistreatment in the #MeToo movement of the past two years have offered, at best, partial acknowledgments. Some (like Matt Lauer) have disputed details. Others (like Harvey Weinstein) have denied any nonconsensual contact. More recently, following a *New York Times* report of singer-songwriter Ryan Adams's mistreatment of several women, he tweeted something that resembled an apology. It contained the words "I apologize," but they followed the words "however unintentionally" and preceded his denials of multiple elements of the accusers' stories.[23] Of course, if a man is innocent of the charges leveled at him, he should defend himself. But none of the accused headliners have offered much in the way of specific, exculpatory information. Neither has one made a thorough, sincere apology. Altogether, I'd say they've offered a clinic on how *not* to make amends. In the coming chapters, we will look at some very effective—even stellar—public apologies, but they are not the rule (yet).

It's not surprising, really, given all our cultural, biological, and social stumbling blocks, that many people don't know how to fix things when they go wrong. It can feel bewildering, discouraging, and down-right impossible.

Do not despair. Despite these challenges, there's nothing more important to learn than how to repair harm. Chapter 3 will show you that it can be done.

APOLOGY MYTHS

Following are some of the most popular misconceptions about the nature of apologies. Do you recognize your own resistance in any of these ideas?

1. An apology is a sign of weakness.
2. Saying "I'm sorry" means you accept the blame. Because you were not at fault, you shouldn't apologize.
3. Taking responsibility for harmful mistakes will get you sued.
4. If you didn't intend to hurt someone, they aren't hurt.
5. Your partner knows you wouldn't hurt them on purpose, so there's no need to say anything about it.
6. You're a nice person, so you couldn't have done anything that hurts someone.
7. Saying "I'm sorry" is all you have to do.
8. Good relationships don't need apologies. ("Love means never having to say you're sorry.")
9. Feeling guilty about mistakes is pointless.
10. Making an apology doesn't benefit you. It only helps the person who's hurt.
11. If the harm happened before you were born, you don't owe anyone an apology for it.
12. "Let sleeping dogs lie." Raising difficult subjects just makes everyone uncomfortable.
13. You can't change the past, so there's no reason to revisit it.
14. You've been hurt, too, so you don't have to be the one to apologize.

CHAPTER 3

It's Not Easy,
but It's Not Mysterious

Jackie, a dedicated social worker in her late thirties, came to see me because she'd been unhappy for a long time—not deeply depressed but lonely. She had a wide circle of acquaintances but very few really close connections. She'd been in a handful of romantic relationships, but none had lasted longer than a few months. Early in her therapy, Jackie told me, "I don't know what my problem is. I can't let anyone in, really." Indeed, she and I discovered her reluctance to trust me, too: She didn't expect me to return her calls, nor to remember what she'd told me about her life. Once, when I offered to rearrange my schedule slightly to accommodate her, she was surprised and uncomfortable. "I'm not used to someone doing something like that for me. I'm usually the one who goes out of my way for other people."

As a child, Jackie had learned not to depend on anyone's help. She'd always been the easygoing sister, the one who got by with very little attention or help. She never felt as if anyone had her back. She'd learned to take care of her own needs. Now, as an adult, Jackie didn't demand anything of anyone in her family and no one focused on her. She often helped out her older sister Serena by picking up her children or babysitting when Serena and her husband went out. Her brothers called her when they needed help, usually financial.

In therapy, she began to explore her family story and recognized for the first time the extent of overt neglect she'd experienced from her single mother. The first time she told me about being sent as a young child to live with a distant cousin named Marian, she told me that the long period away from home "wasn't so bad" because she and Serena were there together. As adults, the sisters had a friendly relationship, with frequent conversations about their work and Serena's children. Serena was known as a kind and gentle person, so Jackie questioned why she never quite trusted her. She figured it was probably due to her own limitations. More than most people I've treated, Jackie worked hard not to blame any of her difficulties on her family, scrupulously taking responsibility herself.

One Saturday during a chatty phone conversation, Serena mentioned that she'd invited their brothers and mother to her house for Easter. She told Jackie that they would have dinner at two because that worked for everyone. Immediately, Jackie could barely speak. She felt that she had to get off the phone. Over the next few days she found herself growing increasingly enraged at her sister, angrier than she had ever felt before. Although she viewed her feelings as too strong, as inappropriate, she couldn't make them go away. For the first time, she asked to meet me for an extra session. She told me that no one had asked *her* what time *she* could come, but that the timing "worked for everyone," so she must not be someone who mattered. She was always only a second thought. But she also said, "I know Serena's really nice, so she really wouldn't do anything to hurt me." I mentioned that often people hurt someone by mistake and aren't aware of the impact. Jackie decided to go talk to her sister, to "take a chance and try to trust her."

She told Serena that she felt left out of the Easter plans.

It didn't go well.

I didn't find out right away because Jackie canceled her next two appointments. By the time she came in again, she was pale and her eyes were red, swollen, and underscored by deep gray circles. She described being very down and confused. Serena had pooh-poohed her reaction and told her not to be silly, that no one meant to hurt her. Then she'd angrily snapped that Jackie's problem was that she listened to me, her therapist, about their family. Serena went on to say that if Jackie kept talking to me, Serena wouldn't be able to stay connected to her. That's why it had been hard for Jackie to attend her recent sessions.

In their conversation, her sister wasn't able to step up, to recognize the way she'd hurt Jackie about Easter. Her counterattack isn't outside the norm for family reactions when someone begins to change a familiar dynamic, but it still packed a wallop.

Turning her sad eyes directly at me, Jackie spoke slowly. "Why would she do that to me? I feel like somehow I've lost my family."

She gazed down at her hands, listless in her lap. Her eyes filled, but as she talked about her sister's reaction and her own pain, she didn't cry. Her sorrow was interrupted by moments when she scowled and shook her head. She saw her sister's threat as "unfair" and "wrongheaded." Her deep disappointment in Serena's response to her complaint was hard for her to bear, and hard even to witness.

At one point, I asked, "Are these terrible feelings you have today at all familiar? Have you ever felt like this before?"

Jackie was silent for a moment; then the tears finally began to stream down her face, like snowmelt filling a creek in the spring. "In a way, I feel like I've always felt like this. Alone."

She paused, but her tears continued. "Remember I told you about staying with Cousin Marian when I was little? *That's* when I remember feeling this lonely. I was all alone then, too."

I waited while she blew her nose. The tears slowed. "What about Serena?" I asked. "You told me before that she was with you."

"Right." She spoke hesitantly. "It doesn't make sense. I don't understand why I feel as if she was cold to me when we were at Marian's, like she left me really alone." She determined aloud, "She wouldn't be like that to anyone, much less her little sister."

Fortunately, this isn't the end of the story for these two sisters, but this part of their struggle is a painful reminder that a missed chance to make something right between people can cause a lot of pain.

Jackie's sadness ran deep. Temporarily estranged from her sister, she didn't talk to Serena for a few weeks. Although she missed her and her children so much she described it as physically painful, she labeled Serena's behavior as "hostage taking." She was as puzzled by it as she was curious about her memories of childhood loneliness. Because she felt heartbroken, it took all her courage not to comply with her sister's demand, but she tried to trust her sense that Serena's threat wasn't fair. Jackie characterized her own stance as the first time she'd ever really stood up for herself—which made her both proud and anxious. I encouraged her to have faith that she and her sister could resolve this standoff.

Easter came and went. Jackie was miserable.

Serena had failed to take responsibility for what she'd done to her sister, but that wasn't her last chance. Finally, the week after Easter, Serena reached out. On the phone, she told Jackie that she wanted to apologize for more than one thing. With some trepidation but with more relief, Jackie agreed to meet her. On a long walk, Serena began by saying she was sorry for being so insensitive about Easter. She hadn't treated her sister with the consideration she deserved. She went on: "I also need to say I'm really sorry for how I reacted to you when you raised the subject. That was wrong, too."

Jackie felt awkward, thanked her quickly, and started to move on to another topic. Those apology statements were all she needed to let the whole thing go. Her response demonstrates that, even though Serena hadn't apologized when she first had an opportunity, often, someone you hurt remains very receptive to another try.

"But there's something else," Serena continued. "I've been thinking about how I reacted to you. Last week when Mom was at my house, I was watching her with the kids and it came to me why I acted like that. I want to tell you, but it's stuff I hadn't thought about for a long, long time." She stopped for a moment before continuing. "You remember when we stayed with Cousin Marian?"

Jackie's surprise made her speechless. It seemed like such an unlikely coincidence, Serena bringing up the same time period she'd been puzzling about with me. She nodded.

"Well, you probably don't know that before we went, Mom made us promise not to talk to Marian—or anyone, for that matter—about anything that went on at our house. You were too little to remember and it was my job to make sure you kept your mouth shut. Mom said she would punish both of us if you spoke up."

"Wow, that's harsh."

"Seriously harsh. Not so out of character with the rest of her parenting, though. Anyway, we'd been there about three months and summer was ending. You were about to start kindergarten. For some reason, you told Marian about how Mom used to get all dressed up at night and go out. Later on, she called Mom and read her the riot act. I heard her yelling on the phone."

"Uh-oh."

"Right. Then Mom asked her to give me the phone. She was furious!" Serena took a deep breath. "Mom told me that we couldn't come home, that we had to stay there for another whole year."

"Oh my God. Is *that* why we stayed there so long?"

"Well, that's how I remember it. She punished us because you spoke up."

"I had no idea—"

"I have to tell you something else, something I hate to say out loud: I was so mad at you that we couldn't go home! I remember that I made a vow not to help you anymore. Not even to be nice to you."

Jackie stared sharply at her sister.

They walked in silence until Serena said, "I had forgotten all about it. You might not remember either, because you were so young."

Jackie whispered, "I do remember." Then, slowly: "It's the same way I felt last month when you told me I couldn't talk to Molly."

Serena wrapped her arms around her sister and they rocked and hugged each other, Serena repeating, "I'm so sorry. I'm so sorry."

The sisters began a conversation that day that continued for many years. Jackie told her sister all about her sense of aloneness. For her, the apology helped unravel the mystery of where her memories and some of her loneliness came from. After remembering her childhood coldness, Serena struggled to forgive herself, but Jackie didn't have any trouble forgiving her. She realized that they were both children whose disturbed parent had put them in an impossible situation. They both had done the best they could.

From Serena's attempt to repair the harm she'd done, a new relationship became possible for the sisters. Serena no longer took her sister for granted, which changed the way the whole family operated. For Jackie, a new and deeper capacity for closeness grew from her sister's apology.

My patients have taught me much of what I know about making amends. In the thousands of hours I've sat with them, I've often heard about the long-standing, stuck places people haven't been able to get past. These painful knots usually involve old hurt that hasn't been healed. But even if you've been stuck for years with accumulated guilt or regret, people have shown me that you can nonetheless learn how to shift the story. You can change the outcome for yourself and your loved ones.

In many instances, poor apologies can be so obviously inadequate that you don't need to be a psychologist to see it. But I've also learned from people who apologize well. I've witnessed partners dropping their defenses and working hard to make up for their regrettable behavior. Although I didn't have anything to do with Serena's making things right with her sister, I heard about how comprehensive and caring her words were. She gave Jackie plenty of time to tell her how she felt, and she made sure that Jackie knew she understood. I witnessed the freeing and transformative power of her courageous apology in Jackie's life.

Her sister's amends allowed Jackie to move on, not only to be more present in her relationship with Serena, but also to flower more fully in the rest of her life. Serena, too, found the apology profound in its effects. About six months after their walk, Jackie brought in a letter from her sister. Addressed to me, the letter was another apology of sorts. In it, Serena related how wrong she had been to threaten Jackie's therapy and thanked me for my support of her sister. "I'm so grateful to have Jackie in my life. We are so much closer now." She went on to tell me how, personally, she has begun to pay a different kind of attention to her children and especially her husband. She's found herself more curious and open to his point of view. She wrote, "I think I've been stuck for a long time in a lot of ways and now I'm becoming more like the person I want to be."

Because Serena faced her regrets with her sister, a relationship that might have been lost was not only saved but improved. She also helped herself grow. When two people create the kind of psychological safety we heard about in Chapter 1—that is, they tell each other the truth about negative or hard things, without doing harm—I often see a release from previous stubborn patterns, those interactions that play like inevitable story lines on a loop. Naturally, the fresh perspective allows people to see more clearly what they love in their relationships and in their partners. The thing about favorable change is that it is energizing, providing momentum to a pair of people to continue positive cycles of behavior. A positive cycle is one where you appreciate the other's efforts or kindness and, as a result, feel more inspired or at least inclined to express your good wishes in actions, too. Both of you feel happier, and that makes you more likely to continue to do the things that make the other person feel good. So, instead of mutual bitterness or negative cycles, you're doing what I call "filling the reservoir of positive feeling," which you might need to tap at some point in the future. You also create a blueprint for future repairs. Particularly in a long relationship, this shared tool kit for communicating and problem solving benefits everyone.

Over time, as I sat with people, especially couples, consistent patterns in what constitutes an effective apology began to emerge. I am not an academic psychologist, so I don't conduct controlled experimental research. But I was curious about how particular apology efforts seemed to work and how powerful they could be. So I went looking for ways to understand what I was seeing. In many divergent places, some of which might surprise you, I've found meaningful ideas about how to make things right. In this chapter, we'll revisit what I learned. These examples further convinced me of the importance of relationship repair and helped inform my apology model.

RELIGIOUS MODELS FOR ADDRESSING REMORSE

The etymology of the word "religion" itself is *re-ligare*, to tie together or connect again. One interpretation of that meaning is that the purpose of religion is to reconnect you with your truest self, the divine, or the rest of your community after you have become separated, as by sin. In this view, mending, reconnecting, and joining back together something broken are central aspects of a religious or spiritual life. Indeed, the Ignatian (Jesuit) Spiritual Exercises go a step further, following an explicit path toward understanding the ways you have become separated from God. From a different perspective, Jews believe that you have a sacred obligation to help repair the broken world, a mandate called *tikkun olam*. The Torah teaches that humans were created to repair the errors that came about in the imperfect creation of the world.

I was particularly interested to discover that rituals for repentance in major religious traditions are ubiquitous, suggesting that the human need to address wrongdoing is almost universal. Across cultures and millennia, religions provide the faithful with routes to repentance.

Through rituals and days set aside for atonement, religions require their adherents to spend time in self-reflection, as on the annual Jewish High Holiday of Yom Kippur. During the Muslim atonement ritual *tawba*, sincere regret leads to turning away from past misdeeds and toward Allah's ways. Sincere remorse is also called for in the Chinese Buddhist process of repentance, which is a way to cleanse negative karma and purify one's mind.

On Ash Wednesday, which for Christians marks the beginning of Lent, the priest's thumb makes the sign of the cross with ashes on the foreheads of the faithful. The charcoal smudge stays all day, worn on one's face as a sign of penitence, humility, and mortality. In the Book of Common Prayer, used by Episcopalians, the Ash Wednesday liturgy announces a season of self-examination and repentance.[1]

But in most of these religions, penitence alone is not sufficient. In Roman Catholicism, the sacrament of confession requires a penitent person to acknowledge sins or errors and express remorse aloud. Similarly, during the ten days between Rosh Hashanah and Yom Kippur, Jews have the obligation to face wrongdoing directly. Personal statements of regret to people you may have harmed must be made during these holy days, before God closes the Book of Life for another year.

Some form of restitution is often required in a religious repentance process. For example, if you've made a Roman Catholic confession, your acknowledgment of sins must be followed by an assigned penance, usually consisting of specific numbers of particular prayers you must say. Likewise, the Jewish confession prayer Ashamnu doesn't immediately bring resolution; it marks a time after which a person can demonstrate the avoidance of future transgressions and thereby show whether he or she deserves forgiveness. Similarly, although the Islamic practice of *tawba* is only between the faithful person and Allah, if you've sinned against another person, restitution is also required.[2]

Saying words of regret or even making restitution does not complete an apology between people, either. Atonement, acknowledgment of wrongs, and restitution set the stage for genuine change in the person who's done something wrong. To me, this seems to be the ultimate purpose of repentance rituals. Going forward, devout Muslims must be determined to forsake prohibited actions. After remorse for past wrongdoing, Chinese Buddhists must change their future behavior.[3] Furthermore, one of the Buddhist sutras (canonical scriptures) proposes six lifelong repentance practices of the senses, mind, and body.[4]

All these rituals and beliefs give people's guilt and responsibility a voice and also gives them a way to repent and start over. Basic to the practices I've described here is a penitent's return to a spiritual source. Generally, though not always, explicit recognition of brokenness is a central part of the shared understanding. In these ways, faith communities can be places where a person is encouraged to face and recover from mistakes that cause breaches of one sort or another. In many traditions, specific reckonings with wronged people are integrated into these practices.

BUSINESS MODELS

When I began my quest to understand repairs between people, I didn't know much about current thinking in the field of business leadership. But some of the most fascinating education I've encountered has been this extensive, creative study of organizations and how people function within work groups. For example, Patrick Lencioni, the management thinker who teaches about the value of intrateam conflict, advocates that business leaders encourage conversations about disagreements.[5] Further, one way to handle thorny emotional complications with coworkers is to face directly the ways you might have caused a problem—which turns out to be a crucial aspect of my apology model.

Leaders must model being receptive to negative feedback, considering it necessary information that will help the team or company thrive. To that end, Kim Scott, a former tech executive and high-profile management consultant, recommends "radical candor," which is not just willingness to tolerate unpleasant words, but an active seeking of differences of opinion. I've found just such an active inquiry to be an essential part of a personal apology. For most leaders, feelings, conflicts, and defensiveness arise—just as they do in personal relationships. In her book, Ms. Scott describes a shocking exchange between her new boss, Google cofounder Larry Page, and team leader Matt Cutts. They disagreed about a proposed plan and Mr. Cutts ended up yelling at the boss. As a new employee, Ms. Scott worried that such vehemence would get him fired, but on the contrary, the raised voices did not faze either one of them. They had a productive and collaborative process, which taught her that open, honest disagreement wasn't necessarily dangerous. She doesn't advocate irate outbursts, but their argument helped her develop more resilience herself; she was able to see that there was a productive way through disputes, even passionate ones.[6]

Radical candor requires a commitment to saying what you mean, even when it is a negative assessment of someone's work or, in the case of a relationship, feedback about a negative impact on you. In order to "drive results collaboratively," you must listen, clarify, learn, debate; it's not a dynamic you can reach effortlessly. It requires a version of the same groundwork that is fundamental to a strong relationship. Even when passions and pressures run high, you must remain committed to being trustworthy, that is, honest, and, despite disagreements, essentially on the same side.

DIGITAL AND COMMUNITY MODELS

Twelve-step programs are semi-secular groups that focus a large amount of attention on making things right with people who've been harmed. In Alcoholics Anonymous's Step 4, the alcoholic must prepare by making a "searching and fearless moral inventory" of personal failings. Focusing on the harms you caused others is a painful process, directly analogous to the religious rituals of repentance. As such, it can form the base for making amends with other people, which comes in AA's Step 9.[7]

Ubiquitous online "confession pages" at colleges and high schools provide a place for young people to post their secrets of all sorts. Standalone confessional websites come and go but are easy to find. Currently they include accessible names like Confessions.net, MomConfessions.net, SimplyConfess.com, and thefutureofsecrets.com. They give people a place to send their stories of remorse. Whether you are a mother who feels bad about your parenting or a lover who has secretly betrayed your partner, you can make a semipublic apology by joining a Facebook group or posting in response to digital calls for stories of wrongdoing. In a more spiritual vein, Harvard Hillel, the Jewish on-campus community, invited students to tweet their sins in preparation for Yom Kippur.[8]

When Frank Warren solicited postcards bearing secrets that hadn't been told to anyone, he wasn't expecting the huge influx of cards he received. Since 2004, he's received more than a million secrets, produced a bestselling series of *PostSecret* books, and hosts an ongoing community art project online. Many of the stories he's received are of a confessional sort, admitting actions (or nonactions) that are regretted.[9]

Another, communal experience of addressing regrets occurs in New York City. On the first day of a new year, people are invited to write down their regrets on pieces of paper. Giant paper shredders are dragged into Times Square, offering the chance for cathartic release of regrets. It's not an interpersonal apology, but it does allow people a ritualized, shared way to acknowledge wrongdoing.

It should be noted that these measures are not real apologies, in that they're rarely directed at someone you've hurt. There is less risk to the writer or poster and almost no follow-up with subsequent steps. What is it that appeals to people about making revelations that are simultaneously anonymous and intensely personal? Why do these opportunities for one-way confessions keep showing up? They must meet a need. I wonder if what we need is the presence of witnesses, even if they're unknown to us. When the departing Pope Benedict XVI made his final Ash Wednesday sermon, he said that "the penitential journey cannot be faced alone."[10] He was referring to specific practices within the Roman Catholic Church, but I suggest that we all benefit from having someone to witness our efforts to face disappointment in ourselves, having failed to live up to our highest ideals. To be most powerful, the witness to your apology would be the relevant person, the one you hurt. But, as a culture, it looks like we can use all the opportunities, however partial, we can get.

CULTURAL MODELS

When I described the Western ideal of stoic self-sufficiency, I was referring to a particular model that does not, of course, reflect all the widely divergent attitudes and mores within American or any society. One problem with that model has been its assumption of normalcy; that is, it was supposed to represent a gold standard of adult functioning for everyone. It should be noted that, until the late twentieth century, a preponderance of research about psychological and medical health was conducted on white male subjects. Most of what we have been taught by experts about health was actually based on only part of the population—and didn't do them justice, either.

Early psychoanalytic theory, from Sigmund Freud through the 1960s, viewed human development in a light consistent with this male-based model. Breaking away from infant attachments (separation) and becoming your own person (individuation) were valorized as the major psychological goals of development.[11] The consequence of this theoretical base was that connections with other people were viewed as less important in adulthood. You can imagine, given this perspective, why retaining or repairing interpersonal relationships wasn't viewed as particularly relevant or valuable. With the introduction of more recent theories, including self psychology and relational psychology, both the purpose and the process of growth began to be viewed as richer and more complicated. In particular, we now understand that development crucially involves deep connections with other people—hence the importance of relationship repair. But those shifts in theoretical approach didn't immediately reach into the broader culture. Even as researchers were beginning to understand the centrality of our connections to one another, we were still surrounded by go-it-alone icons like the Marlboro Man.

Many cultural traditions have long provided models of responsible maturity that differ sharply from the familiar independent, masculinized stance; searching for them can help us understand a fuller range of interpersonal options. In my experience, groups that value collective and cooperative approaches support a mind-set better suited to facing your mistakes and resolving differences. Directly challenging the older standard can illuminate more hopeful, positive ways to mend problems between people.

That said, I grew up white in America and am barely beginning to understand cultural models other than that dominant one. Because I don't want to try to speak for those who can speak better for themselves, my words here serve mainly to acknowledge that many people do not ascribe to those prominent European American or masculinized views. Juana Bordas, a multicultural activist, recommends "a new social covenant" that incorporates Latinx, black, and Native American approaches to community. For example, she teaches that generosity within the community, a broader sense of kinship and responsibility to one another, and a deeper commitment to a wider form of family are important values to incorporate into a benevolent and just society.[12]

When we look for them, we find other sources of similar values. As additional ethnic and national groups have become part of the American populace, they've brought with them traditions that honor the group's well-being over the individual's. Also, throughout history, various utopian societies, particularly communes, have espoused collectivism and shared ownership. Feminist analyses of society propose shared, decentralized power as an ideal. Connection with others, responsibility for others, and generosity to others are values we hear about occasionally in the mainstream American press, but usually only as human-interest stories, that is, of secondary interest—not as expressing the central tenets of the culture. Nonetheless, these distinct perspectives persist, offering alternative (and, to my mind, welcome) views of how people live in relation to others.

What do these cultural perspectives have to do with apologies? As the world has grown smaller, in that we are virtually connected all the time, and as we have access to more information and more opinions than ever, somehow we find more reasons to pull apart from one other. Our differences separate and divide us and seem to embody good versus evil, not only us versus them. You might stop talking—and, perhaps more damagingly, stop listening—to people with whom you disagree. You might lose connections with old friends and family members. You might find yourself confident in your rightness, and it might turn out to be a recipe for loneliness. But if we can embrace—or at least borrow—the principles of mutuality and shared responsibility, priorities shift. We find it necessary—and easier—to heal and save our relationships.

A third way. It's arguable, for sure, but it's been said that cosmology and mythology are as much a part of human nature as biology and logic.[13] In ancient myths, the hero faces an opposing power, much as many of us see "our side" facing "the other" across the political or personal divide. But our current sense of division between people doesn't take into account the way the mythical stories often unfold. In old folktales, the drama of two forces at loggerheads at times yields to a surprising, third element. Often the third way was present all along but not seen as a potential solution. The third, simpleton son inherits his father's kingdom after his more intelligent brothers lose battles to each other during their trials; Goldilocks makes two extreme choices before she finds the just-right bed and bowl; and frequently it takes the protagonist three tries to rescue the princess, save her or his brothers, or guess Rumpelstiltskin's name. If you want to borrow from these ancient stories, you can widen your view and look for solutions beyond the initial, win-lose focus that dominates current discourse.

A third way is an alternative or middle ground between two opposing viewpoints. This is an idea that has been applied in arenas as divergent as Thomas Aquinas's cosmological argument for the existence of God[14] and an approach to political economy that sought to find a middle path between capitalism and socialism.[15] For my purposes, a third way is problem solving that preserves the preexisting positions and realities but builds a bridge between them. Neither side wins at the expense of the other. This model resembles compromise—itself extremely valuable—except that, as I understand it, compromise is primarily characterized by concessions.

On occasion, a public figure has been able to tolerate the dissonance between two competing positions or beliefs rather than resolve it by choosing one of the conflicting views. In 1985, Israeli prime minister Shimon Peres found himself in an unpleasant bind in relation to his close ally US president Ronald Reagan. As a gesture of reconciliation with Germany, Mr. Reagan planned to honor World War II casualties buried in a cemetery in Bitburg, Germany. However, it turned out that forty-nine members of the Waffen-SS—people responsible for killing many Jews in the Holocaust—were also buried there. The deeply painful and offensive visit was criticized by many in the United States and Israel. Rather than, for example, deciding that Mr. Reagan was not his ally or changing the widely held view that the Bitburg cemetery visit was disrespectful, Mr. Peres said, "A friend is a friend; a mistake is still a mistake. When a friend makes a mistake, it is still a mistake. And a friend is still a friend. Mr. Reagan remains a friend, but I haven't changed my view."[16] This particular stance resembles a third way in that it preserves two different truths and preserves relationships with flawed (that is to say, *all*) people.

JUSTICE MODELS

Most criminal justice efforts are geared toward punishment, not repair. However, even in the arena of legal proceedings, where defensive counterarguments are de rigueur, there is a place for expressions of remorse. Their impact on court decisions and especially in sentencing can be powerful. The capacity to regret one's actions suggests something about the humanity of the accused and their ability to change and learn. Similarly, an apology marks a turn from harmdoing to rightmaking. Recently, actress Felicity Huffman, one of the wealthy parents accused of cheating to get their children into college, was the first of the Varsity Blues defendants to be sentenced. Unlike many others, she pleaded guilty and made statements in which she accepted culpability and expressed remorse, which may have contributed to her sentence of only two weeks in prison, half the sentence recommended by prosecutors. US attorney Andrew Lelling mentioned her contrition as a factor in her receiving a lighter sentence than some other parents.[17]

In civil proceedings, the plaintiff must be "made whole"; that is, the defendant must make restitution for the loss incurred. In order to hold oneself accountable, an effective personal apology should contain some form of restitution as well.

Restorative justice programs, a growing alternative to standard criminal justice practice, aim toward repair and reparations rather than punishment. Many court systems around the world incorporate restorative practices.[18] What characterizes these processes is that, from the beginning, they include both the victim and the offender. Often, they begin in a meeting that follows a "listening circle" model used in many indigenous cultures (everyone's voice is heard; only one person speaks at a time; all parties have support people present). By the end of the opening circle, the entire group has produced a written contract, signed by all parties. It specifies what the person who caused harm—the "responsible party"—must do in order to make things right for the victim and the community. Almost always, the agreement includes a careful, thorough apology letter, which is delivered to all the affected parties or read at a closing circle, or both.[19] In the United States, ever more states have statutory requirements to refer cases—often those involving youthful or nonviolent offenders—to restorative justice teams, rather than to arraignment.[20] That means the person responsible for the harm is not formally charged, and, if the restorative agreement is satisfied, there is no criminal record.

Michelle Alexander, award-winning author of *The New Jim Crow*, recently reported that more than 90 percent of the survivors of violent crimes in New York City would prefer a justice solution that empowers survivors to help decide how the criminal damage will be repaired. Rather than send the person who harmed them to prison, people who have been shot, stabbed, or robbed would prefer to be heard in a restorative justice circle, get answers from the perpetrators, help devise an accountability plan, and receive victim support services.[21]

Community-based restorative processes, rather than incarceration, may be what best addresses the needs of crime victims. Personal accountability, genuine expressions of hurt and remorse, and thoughtful consideration of restitution are the same tools that I've seen work to help people move through painful relationship situations.

In other social justice arenas, new rules of sensitive engagement have emerged. One is to let the people most affected by the harm determine what amends they need. Another is to affirm that it's almost never too late to make reparations, which can take many creative forms.

MEDICINE MODELS

Partly spurred by the Michigan model's success, but also based on an ethical commitment to handle medical injuries responsibly, several hospitals across the country have adopted their own communication-and-resolution programs. The name of a version adopted by several Massachusetts hospitals explicitly emphasizes the importance of apologizing after an injury: Communication, Apology, and Resolution (CARe).[22]

Early in this movement toward transparency about errors, families and patients who had been hurt were asked what they needed. What they asked for was full disclosure, honest information about what happened, transparent explanations of why it happened, how their harm would be healed, and how recurrences would be prevented. Families weren't looking for someone to blame—or sue. Their needs are directly analogous to the hurt person's interests in my model, the things I encourage an apologizer to address.[23] More recently, researchers have found that patients and families have a strong need to be heard by the medical staff. They were most satisfied when the physicians' communications were empathic and nonadversarial, at all stages of recovery from medical injuries.[24] As in many other contexts, what people who are hurt need is for their pain to be recognized and for those responsible for it to own up and make things right.

PUBLIC APOLOGY MODELS

Public apologies are not the same as the private moments between partners, but the same framework often applies. Individuals and couples may be able to learn something from successful public statements, and those in the spotlight can learn something from what works between two people. Just as with personal apologies, public ones must corroborate facts of the victims' experience.[25] To be effective, you have to admit to the hurtful behavior and express regret to the person(s) harmed.

Sometimes, an apology is most effective when made to a large, public audience. In an interview, Jason Alexander, an actor best known for portraying George on the sitcom *Seinfeld*, made jokes about the sport of cricket being "a bit gay." At first, he didn't see why his Twitter followers were offended. But after he spent time asking other people to help him understand the impact of his statement, he began to realize his error. He issued a thorough public apology in which he articulated the problem: By building his jokes on the premise that effeminate is the equivalent of gay, he "added to the pejorative stereotype [gay people] are forced to deal with every day." In addition, he said that he played into hurtful assumptions that lead to all kinds of abuse and that he "should know better." He took full responsibility for his mistake.[26]

On a much larger scale, some of the most impressive apologies have been public ones made on behalf of an entire community or country. While there is a ceremonial aspect to them, such words of regret are nonetheless important ones to speak and to hear, in the service of healing. When actions or policy changes accompany the words, though, they take on even greater significance. For example, Germany has engaged in ongoing efforts toward post–World War II reconciliation. Konrad Adenauer, the first postwar chancellor of West Germany, was reportedly driven by moral guilt to begin a reparations process with Israel that led, among other things, to compensation and restitution for individual Jews. He offered a "solution of the material indemnity problem, thus easing the way to the spiritual settlement of infinite suffering." This is an example of monetary restitution that serves both as real reparation and as a symbolic step toward reconciliation.

Sites of Nazi crimes such as concentration camps now serve as teaching centers, and in Berlin many physical reminders mark the locations of arrests and former homes of those terrorized by the Third Reich. A scholar at the American Institute for Contemporary German Studies, Lily Gardner Feldman, PhD, says that reconciliation efforts continue and that, still today, people are reclaiming art seized by the

Nazis and monitoring textbooks for correct historical reports and language.[27] She characterizes Germany's reconciliation process as "long, messy and...not yet ended."[28] The efforts go on, as one family at a time experiences a form of reconciliation that is tangible and the memory of harm is kept in the public consciousness.

Closer to home, President Ronald Reagan finally apologized to Japanese Americans for their internment during World War II. After considerable resistance, he signed the formal statement called the Civil Liberties Act of 1988. Based on years of study by a congressional commission, the act provided for acknowledgment of injustice, public apology, financial restitution, and public education to prevent a recurrence of this kind of harm. John Tateishi, a leader of the Japanese American Citizens League, which worked for a decade to reach this conclusion, said that the redress campaign was less about the compensation itself than about the next generation. He quoted the Japanese saying *kodomo no tame ni*, which means "for the sake of the children." He emphasized that the correction of a historical mistake should include the legacy of not repeating it.[29]

One example of widely viewed public education was the 1987 Smithsonian Museum of American History exhibit *A More Perfect Union: Japanese Americans and the US Constitution*. Viewing it with my children in the 1990s was the first time I encountered much of the story about the displacement and internment. As many as 120,000 people, 75,000 of whom were US citizens, were incarcerated.

In 1992, an amendment added more funds to support the commitments made in the 1988 legislation. In addition to the financial redress delivered to 82,219 people, a Civil Liberties Public Education Fund provided for 135 projects, including documentaries, podcasts, teachers' guides, and community discussions.[30] A California Civil Liberties Program carries on the effort by funding similar projects to ensure that the events surrounding the removal and incarceration are remembered and their causes understood and prevented from recurring.[31]

It's Not Easy, but It's Not Mysterious

* * *

Despite his more recent, complicated public relations, a current leader who has repeatedly demonstrated the steps of a good apology is Canadian prime minister Justin Trudeau. For example, in 2018 he made an emotional statement to Parliament in which he itemized in detail the government's harmful actions toward LGBTQ2 citizens. Repressive policies that began during the Cold War and continued into the 1990s destroyed many people's lives and amounted to a "gay purge." After each offense he listed, he repeated "I am sorry" and "We are so very sorry" with evident feeling. His speech was accompanied by financial recompense to survivors and their families, as well as changes in laws.[32]

A crucial lesson we can learn from Mr. Trudeau is how to say "I'm sorry" without complicating the message. As one observer, Liberal MP Rob Oliphant, a gay man, described, "There was no equivocation. There was no justification. There was no, 'Well, we didn't know things that we know now.'" Another witness, former naval officer Todd Ross, who's been involved in a related class-action lawsuit, said, "It was something I needed to hear." He went on: "It marks the beginning of healing for many people."[33]

Mr. Trudeau also personified taking responsibility on behalf of his country when he expressed apparently sincere regret and empathy to those harmed in other groups, including First Nations peoples and passengers aboard the MS *St. Louis*—refugees from Nazism who were turned away by Canada and other countries.[34] More than 250 of those 900 asylum seekers died in death camps; only one, Ana Maria Gordon, lives in Canada today. She and her family attended Mr. Trudeau's address in 2018 and met privately with him.

Underscoring the value of a good, thorough apology, Ms. Gordon's son Danny Gruner stated, "You will not remove the guilt from the perpetrators of the horror. But at least you can come to terms with what the country was at the time and try to understand...where we want to be."[35] This is the change we want to effect when we express our regrets: to help the hurt one(s) heal and to create the possibility of a better future.

PUTTING IT ALL TOGETHER

Apologies are not only possible, but also among the most basic of human actions. The examples I've found in other domains encouraged me to pull all these elements together into a model that would make them more widely accessible. Despite the challenges, anyone can do this hard thing.

We begin with the awareness that everyone makes mistakes, hurts people, or commits wrongdoing in one form or another—whether knowingly or unintentionally. From this, it follows that, at some point, we all have reason to feel remorse. It might surprise you to hear that guilt, regret, and remorse are crucially important aids in this repair work. Contrary to common wisdom, they are not useless, even harmful, emotions that serve only to make people feel bad about themselves. As we saw earlier, guilt certainly can cause a person trouble, but that's true only if it's unaddressed. On the contrary, what I call "good guilt" can be productive because it makes you uncomfortable enough to do something about it. When you do wrong, you feel a not-so-gentle pricking that telltales itself into consciousness and requires reckoning. Good guilt fits the offense, makes sense, and is what you ought to feel when you do something bad. It's one way you know you've done wrong. It's one way you know you're a good person. Good guilt drives the possibility of repair.

In a recent study of incarcerated men, Dr. June Tangney found that those who reported more guilt feelings turned out to be much less likely to re-offend in the first year following release. In a different study, she found that both men and women who feel more guilt are also more empathic, that is, able to feel for other people.[36]

It should be noted that this productive guilt (what Buddhists call "wise remorse"[37]) operates quite differently from shame. Many psychologists make a fundamental distinction between guilt, which is feeling bad about something you've done, and shame, which is feeling bad about who you are. The two arise along distinct developmental paths and can lead to quite different outcomes. Shame tends to motivate people to hide, escape, deny, or sometimes blame another person. According to bestselling author and research professor Brené Brown, shame correlates positively with many serious mental health and social disorders, whereas guilt is inversely related to the same problems.[38] Shame, that most wasteful of emotions, rarely leads to effective repairs, whereas guilt can lead to genuine accountability.

In order to recover from wrongdoing and repair damage you've caused, I recommend holding yourself and others accountable, while remaining humane. I try to cultivate this "compassionate accountability" in my patients—and in myself. Feelings of self-condemnation can be counterproductive, but so can defensive denials of responsibility. I propose that we rigorously address our errors and our negative impacts on other people. Coming to terms with the need to make amends requires that you both strengthen your resolve and soften your pride, which can seem like a daunting combination of courage and humility, but it's not beyond what most people can do.

I developed my four-step apology model to address the natural, timeless desire to make things right—and the confusion most of us have about how to do that. The method presented in this book begins as an invitation to another person, not a demand.

In the upcoming chapters, you will learn how to apologize, step-by-step. (See the box at the end of this chapter for a list.) However, if you're reading this book in hopes of a quick solution to a thorny inter-personal problem, you may be disappointed. These steps take time. They take patience. Ours is not a patient age, but the kinds of feeling, listening, and responding that lead to resolution take human time, not digital time. Quick responses rarely heal hurt between people.

The chapters ahead will present each of the four essential steps of a good apology, all of which are necessary for true healing.

THE FOUR STEPS OF A GOOD APOLOGY

First, you must come to understand the other person's injury, including the effects of your actions. This usually involves asking questions and listening.

Second, you must articulate a sincere statement of regret. You must acknowledge what you did and how it affected the other person. This is no small feat for most of us, especially when we didn't intend to hurt someone.

Third, you must make reparations. This can include material restitution, although in relationships that's less likely to occur.

Fourth, you must make a convincing plan to prevent the problem from happening again.

PART II

HOW TO APOLOGIZE

CHAPTER 4

Step One: Don't Just Do Something; Stand There

Even though we refer to "saying 'I'm sorry,'" the first step in an effective apology doesn't involve *saying* anything. It involves listening.

The purpose of Step One is to listen carefully to someone else, so you can learn how that person has been hurt. It's not a time to share your reasons or explanations, or your benign intentions or countercomplaints. It's not about alleviating your guilt or shame or any feelings you, the would-be apologizer, have.

If you want to apologize, Step One is not about you at all. It's only about understanding the other person's experience of hurt.

Margo, a stylish middle-aged woman, came into my office carrying a small sheaf of papers. I hadn't seen her for twelve years, since she sought help with the emotional aftermath of her divorce. During that therapy, she got herself back on her psychological feet and wasn't interested in further exploration. This time, she described a puzzling and vexing situation with her close friend Annie, who wouldn't or couldn't forgive her for something, "even though I've said 'I'm sorry'!" I remembered hearing about Annie's supportiveness throughout Margo's divorce and had even met her once in the waiting room when she'd driven Margo in. The two had been very close, planning, half in jest, to live together "as old ladies," after they outlived their husbands.

A competent professional who spoke directly and with confidence, Margo described how confused and irritated she was by her friend's "stonewalling" her. Six months earlier, Margo had temporarily broken off contact with Annie, after insensitive remarks by a third friend were followed by silence from Annie. Acknowledging an old pattern, Margo said that she'd been feeling hurt and overwhelmed for months about other aggravations before she "took the coward's way out" and emailed her intention to take a break from the relationship. Annie immediately reached out and tried to repair the problem, which incensed Margo because she felt that her friend didn't honor her initial request for no communication. I read the email exchanges, including Annie's "disrespectful" second email in which she wrote that she was finding the unpredictable break terribly hard because of her own painful history. (I had heard years ago that, as a young adult, soon after the death of her parents, she had been abruptly abandoned by her extended family.) Margo's escalating fury was evident in her strong email language. When Annie replied with a warm apology and a request to maintain some minimal connection, Margo threatened to "lock my doors and windows if you dare to come to my house." She blocked her on all media.

Margo seemed to believe she had simply taken charge of a bad situation and taken care of herself. Maybe she had come in so I could help her see what she was missing. My thudding heart alerted me that Margo may have hurt her friend more than she had let herself know.

After months without contact, Margo's anger about previous hurts and Annie's "hounding" her had cooled. She had then texted Annie a friendly, upbeat message that concluded, "Can we get together soon? I miss you!" She'd expected her friend to be relieved and glad to be in touch again. But her response had been only a brief "Thank you." After Margo emailed, "I'm sorry for our 'break,' but you know how upset I was," Annie didn't reply for an entire week. Then she wrote, "I don't know what to do about getting together. Maybe we should talk first, to figure out how to do that or set some guidelines or something."

Surprised and uncertain what she should do, Margo came to see me and relayed the story. The second time we met, Margo brought in Annie's latest email, which said, "I'm just not ready to see you, as if nothing happened."

Margo was mystified. "I don't get it. I know distancing myself isn't always the best way to handle conflict, but I already said 'I'm sorry' for it. What more does she want from me?"

That was the right question, an opening for me. "Saying you're sorry is a good step, but something else has to happen, too."

YOU HAVE TO ASK AND LISTEN

After a misstep, the first, automatic thing some of us do is say, "I'm sorry." We hope that's the end of it. The "magic words" spoken aloud can be delivered as if fulfilling a requirement, reluctant and resented code words that signal the end of a standoff or of a power struggle. But even when "I'm sorry" is a sincere attempt to repair a relationship, it isn't enough.

One obvious drawback to saying those words before fully understanding the actual injury is that you might not apologize for the correct thing. Comedian Louis C.K. made this mistake after he was first accused in 2017 by several women of sexual misconduct. Initially, he tried to apologize to the wrong woman for the wrong offense. When he subsequently offered a plan to spend a lot of time listening, he had the right idea. (We later learned that, unfortunately, he may not have listened much then, either.)

Listening is essentially receptive—and many of us find it more comfortable to take action than to remain patient and silent. Step One can be much harder than saying the words "I'm sorry." *Asking* for another person's perspective on your impact can make you feel more vulnerable than *saying* anything. When you ask someone to tell you about their hurt, you put yourself in a position to hear things you hadn't been aware of—because of your error blindness—and no one enjoys that kind of news. Moreover, the feedback you receive may make you feel guilty or ashamed. Just thinking about it can make you feel defensive and uncomfortable; reluctance to engage in this step can become a major barrier to apologizing well.

Further, when you ask for this kind of information, you are also likely to open yourself up to feeling for the other person, empathically. Altogether, such a lot of feeling and complexity may seem unappealing, unwelcome. The temptation to skip this step is understandable. However, it is the base on which everything else is built.

The task is to put our defensive reluctance aside, in order to reconnect.

In their friendship, Margo and Annie hadn't yet established psychological safety, the climate in which it's not only okay but desirable to give the other feedback, including negative information about the other's effect on you. We need help to fully understand how we affect each other because, as we've discussed, we humans are very poor at recognizing our own errors and their impact. Margo knew what she'd done, but she didn't appreciate the effect she'd had on her friend. Like many, she not only was unaware of what the other person experienced; she also didn't know how to find out.

A common misconception suggests that just thinking about another person and trying to take her or his point of view will produce understanding. This strategy is fine for some purposes (increasing altruism, decreasing stereotyping), but even if you are remarkably intuitive, your guessing has big limitations. It turns out that accurately comprehending another person's point of view takes more than imagination. It requires getting real information that can be obtained only by asking that person.

In a 2018 report based on twenty-five studies of almost three thousand people, researchers found that individuals who attempted to take someone else's perspective were *less* accurate—although they sometimes had increased confidence in their "knowledge." Experimenters asked people to identify the thoughts, feelings, and preferences of other people, ranging from complete strangers to spouses. Whether they guessed the emotions of other people from photographs or videos, or predicted which activities their partners would like or which opinions they'd endorse, those who were encouraged specifically to first try to take the other person's point of view were less accurate than people who just guessed. The researchers concluded that, even with people you know well, imagining someone else's experience doesn't help you get it right. In order to identify another's viewpoint, you have to ask them. The authors called it "perspective-getting," which you would accomplish by inquiring, over "perspective-taking" on your own.[1]

The goal here is greater common understanding and empathy. As the author and essayist Leslie Jamison writes, "Empathy requires inquiry as much as imagination. Empathy requires knowing you know nothing."[2] With a familiar person, asking can help you learn about their perspective on relationship events you might not have noticed. Such knowledge may help you grow closer and, together, find ways to challenge long-standing patterns. In order to understand what happened between them, Margo would have to ask Annie.

The difficulty most of us have understanding the perspectives of other people contributes to a larger problem of polarization across political and social differences. We don't know how the "other side" thinks, and too often we don't express curiosity in order to understand better. We don't seem to know that we don't know. If we want to see across the divide, Peter Wehner, senior fellow at the conservative think tank Ethics and Public Policy Center, recommends "epistemological modesty."[3] That is, we should recognize how much we don't know about other people.

Because we are often off base about other people's experience and are poorly equipped to see our mistakes, we need others to tell us when we err. As with driving, we can't avoid blind spots in our view, but in order to be responsible drivers, we must take our blind spots into account and actively look out for them. If you're lucky enough to have people you trust, you can ask for their help with this. As a kindness, they can offer you the information you need about how you affect them—and you can offer the same to them. That's one way of creating the condition of psychological safety we've been talking about.

Unfortunately, other people usually don't give us spontaneous feedback on our interpersonal mistakes. In one recent Harvard Business School study, coworkers could easily identify slights directed at them, such as backhanded compliments, but rarely informed the people who made the comments.[4] A similar pattern occurs in families, among friends, and even in therapy. In many circumstances, people tend to avoid criticizing one another, afraid of hurting feelings, inviting backlash, or sounding judgmental. We miss lots of chances to learn due to what others don't tell us and what we don't ask about.

In addition to the trouble we all have detecting our missteps, one research report suggests that men may have an even harder time seeing their mistakes than women do. A recent controlled study led by the California Institute of Technology, Wharton School, Western University, and ZRT Laboratory examined the effects of testosterone on human cognition and decision-making. Studying hundreds of men, the researchers found that higher testosterone levels decreased a subject's ability to discern flaws in his thinking, which led to overconfidence. This finding suggests that it may behoove men, even more than women, to make purposeful inquiries into how they've made other people feel.[5] Of course, as Margo demonstrates, women aren't exempt from hurting people without realizing it, either.

LISTENING

So how do we learn to ask for feedback, listen honestly, and ultimately understand another person's perspective? Early in my career, when I was introduced to self psychology, I was somewhat resistant. This is the theory of psychotherapy I mentioned earlier, the approach that requires a therapist to be radically empathic to patients. I understood that, within the therapeutic process, a person might feel hurt or disappointed, for example, by a therapist's incomplete or incorrect understanding (the "empathic failure" that is an almost inevitable part of therapy). But my initial reaction to the idea of focusing openly on how I'd hurt my patient was defensive: Not only had I not meant to hurt anyone, I hadn't done anything technically "wrong." Indeed, the patient's hurt feelings often occurred within what psychologists call the transference relationship—that is, the responses weren't solely about me, but about someone important in the person's past. To me, sometimes they seemed the result of oversensitivity. For two years, my supervisors at Beth Israel Hospital (now called Beth Israel Deaconess Medical Center), particularly psychologist Betty North, and I went over session notes in great detail. They helped me learn how to hold people's experiences of injury openly, gently, and fully. We found that many hurts could in fact be faced together and healed. According to self psychology thinker Heinz Kohut, the repair of relational harm (if it's not too great) is essential for growth.[6]

I didn't yet know how this practice of careful listening would inform my apology method, but its deliberate, receptive listening came to mind a decade later when I encountered psychologist Harville Hendrix's approach to couples communication. In his workshops and his book *Getting the Love You Want*, Dr. Hendrix presented a method of painstaking dialogues, in which couples practiced listening to each other and repeating the other's words in order to reinforce what was being said. It's become an influential technique, and I have used it many times in my practice. His system requires a person to mirror a partner's communication, without adding any response of their own: "I heard you say you're bothered by my flirting at company parties. Is that right?" What may feel like tedious dialogue slows down the interaction, which limits emotional reactivity and makes escalation of an argument less likely.[7]

But, to my mind, the primary benefit of Hendrix's technique is that the pair maintains focus on the initial speaker's words, not the listener's potential replies. There are so many possible ways to head off unwelcome feedback about ourselves, about our mistaken, insensitive, or otherwise regrettable behavior. ("I didn't mean it like that." "I wouldn't do anything to hurt you." "I was only kidding.") Many of them have to do with protecting a treasured self-concept. For example, if I believe I am a nice person (or a good therapist), the idea that I've done something that hurt your feelings presents a challenge to my sense of myself. One common type of response is to reject the message, sometimes before it's fully delivered. ("Wait a second, that's not what I meant!" "I didn't say that!" "You're taking this out of context.") It seems like the other person must be mistaken, misinterpreting, oversensitive.

The thing is, you don't have to change your mind about yourself to listen to someone else's experience of your actions. You don't even have to believe that you actually caused harm. But you do have to learn to focus fully on another person during a discussion of how they've been affected.

Hearing another person's experience of harm is powerful for the listener who would like to understand, but it can be of even greater value to the one whose story is heard. In itself, having one's truth known and acknowledged is profound, whether the harm is small and personal or enormous and nationwide.

HEAR THE HURT

A public process that stands out as a beacon across the world occurred in South Africa following the fall of apartheid. After many years of the racist and discriminatory system of violent oppression, the new government established a Truth and Reconciliation Commission, which gave those who'd been mistreated the chance to tell—and hear—their stories of harm. The power of having your painful truth heard and known cannot be overstated. The goal was not to punish the perpetrators—who in fact were offered amnesty in exchange for full disclosure—but to acknowledge publicly the harm inflicted and experienced, to provide information to survivors, and potentially to be able to coexist.

Despite the lack of contrition on the part of some perpetrators, more than twenty-one thousand victims came forward and, for the record, presented their experiences of serious harm. According to legal scholar and human rights expert Martha Minow, official recognition of individuals' stories helped to "create a framework for the nation to deal with its past [based on the idea that] telling and hearing the truth is healing."[8] An essential element of this testimony appears to be that those testifying were treated "as persons to be believed, rather than troublemakers or even people with a burden to prove their story."[9] The analogous stance for interpersonal apologies is the assumption that the other person's hurt is real and their report is legitimate. Even the discovery, during the trials, of the terrible details of a loved one's demise allowed for the progression of grief and, potentially, healing.[10]

Earlier, we saw how medical patients who have been harmed

by "adverse events" also have a crucial need to be heard. Translating that need into necessary action steps for doctors, Michigan's Richard Boothman recommended that the first meeting with injured patients and families should consist of *80 percent listening* to them by the staff.[11]

On a more intimate level, creating a safe space to discuss the hurt in a relationship can also begin the process of healing—even well after the offenses occurred. Years after the writer Cris Beam's marriage ended, she still felt penitent about the hurt she'd caused when she'd left her partner. Ms. Beam had previously said she was sorry, but "the words didn't reach the bottom of an experience as deep as abandonment." In a telephone call, her ex-wife told her that she'd never had the opportunity to tell the writer how the pain of being left had affected her.

What Ms. Beam realized is that a key part of the apology she owed her ex-wife was fully listening to her experience, "taking it in deeply." She went to see her in the hope that they could together try to make a better repair. She offered the space to speak and hear, not because it was part of any ritual she knew of, but because she realized that's what she herself had most wanted when she'd been hurt. "Maybe," she wrote, "this was a universal longing—to be listened to, rather than apologized at." The resulting conversation led to deeper understanding of the sadness she'd caused, a more fitting statement of apology, and apparently more healing for the person she'd hurt.[12]

For many, hearing another person's hurt doesn't come easily. On any scale, the skill of listening to and honoring someone else's experience can be challenging. When a patient of mine was telling her husband about how he had hurt her, he kept giving her explanations. She finally said, "You don't get to talk. I'm simply hurt." As with many of us, it was hard for him to understand what she needed. She later told me, "It took him two days to see that I didn't want him to say 'I'm sorry.' I wanted him to know how it feels to be me."

The idea here is that validation of another person's perspective requires listening in an open-minded way, that is, without precon-ceived ideas. Or, as a friend told me, "I don't need my partner to tell me I'm right, but I want him to acknowledge that I'm not crazy."

In the context of constant communications, which occur at light speed, it's harder still to remember principles like receptivity to others' points of view. You may wish for a culture based on dearly held values, like kindness and mutual respect, but, in the heat of the ever-stimulating moment, it's challenging to remain true to your goal. Anecdotal evidence and research data suggest that social media in-flame disagreements and stoke angry responses. Just as you do in the presence of a real person, online you also need to exercise curiosity and listen more than speak if you want a chance to discover unex-pected information.

On the level of a wounded nation and between individuals, peo-ple need their realities to be heard. As hard as it is to take Step One, it's entirely possible. And, along with Margo, you can learn to do it.

Margo and I continued our conversation about what more she could do in her problem situation with Annie. Her arms were crossed as I asked, "Could it be she doesn't feel you really understand how your actions affected her?"

She shook her head quickly. "Oh, come on. I know her feelings were hurt. But mine were, too. Can't she get over it? I did!"

"Yes, you had a way of doing that on your own." I paused. "I'm not challenging your way of dealing with hurt—not yet, anyway—but maybe you two could deal with this standoff more directly, by finding out what this was like for her."

Sometimes asking questions doesn't seem necessary, either be-cause you know the other person well and believe you already know how they feel, or because what you did wrong is obvious, like when you close the door on another person's hand. However, even then, things may be more complicated than you realize.

If you bump into someone by mistake or inconvenience them, a simple expression of regret makes sense and handles the situation immediately. ("Oops, I'm so sorry I stepped on your toes / in front of you in line / into your photograph.") In that case, though, it still could be worth checking back to see if there are any aftereffects. No ill intent was involved, but hurt may nonetheless have happened.

Accidental bumping is a good analogy for what happens when people are close in ways other than physical ones. We bruise one another's sensitive places, step on one another's emotional toes. We may not realize that we've done it.

What Margo wanted was to be reconnected with her old friend. She wanted to be "forgiven" for her retreat. Moreover, she wanted not to have to deal with uncomfortable feelings with her friend. We can all probably relate to those wishes. But they won't repair hurt between people.

Of course, Margo isn't alone in wanting to avoid interpersonal conflict. Despite the high cost of conflict avoidance in many arenas, there is enormous cultural and individual reluctance to tackle difficult interpersonal differences—what popular writer and researcher Brené Brown calls "rumbling with vulnerability."[13]

Margo had to challenge her natural cognitive inclination. She had to ask Annie for information that conflicted with what she knew and believed about what had happened between them. That is really hard to do. Her eventual willingness to be vulnerable and open to criticism—both with me and with Annie—is a form of the "daring greatly" that Dr. Brown says we need if we want to be empathic to another person's experience.[14] In order to approach contentious conversations, or those that carry strong emotions, we must commit ourselves to openness that can at first seem radical. Practice helps.

Step One: Don't Just Do Something; Stand There

YOU WON'T GET IT RIGHT, RIGHT AWAY

Beginning this kind of inquiry also requires us to challenge our perfectionism. Not only did Margo have to consider that she'd caused hurt, which placed her in an unfavorable light. But also, like many people, once she decided to make an apology, Margo had expected herself to be able to deliver a perfect one. Perfectionism is usually defined as having excessively high personal standards and overly critical self-evaluations. According to psychologists Thomas Curran and Andrew Hill, this characteristic has grown in prevalence over the past three decades, possibly due to cultural factors including "competitive individualism," a version of which we introduced in Chapter 2.[15] Believing that you should already be on top of something can interfere with the humble and curious stance that facilitates learning. If you think you should get things right, you're less likely to seek help and less likely to try again if you don't get it right the first time.

Moreover, we resist looking at our mistakes for another, more basic reason. In neuroscientific terms, our brains themselves are driven to be efficient; noticing and correcting an error is way more "work." It costs your brain more energy than just going along uncritically.

The best way to override those limitations may be to focus on a competing wish. For example, although Margo definitely had perfectionistic leanings, her strong wish to reconnect with Annie made her willing to consider my perspective, to question her approach, and to try again, more openly. On a larger scale, political activists such as those in Showing Up for Racial Justice, a nationwide organization dedicated to combating racism, approach perfectionism in much the same way. They make an explicit commitment to "anti-perfectionism," challenging our tendency to let the fear of making a mistake prevent us from trying to address societal wrongs. For example, white activists often take missteps when they try to address issues around race. They say the wrong thing or say it in an "innocently offensive" (my phrase) way.

When made aware of the mistake, many feel inclined to step way back and try to avoid offending anyone or losing face further. Of course, offending isn't a good idea, but the overarching goal requires people working for greater justice to tolerate the discomfort of having made a mistake and try again. The negative feedback is an opportunity to learn how to do better next time.[16]

Margo's first attempt to apologize had been inadequate because she'd employed only Step Two (saying she was sorry) and only partly. No wonder it didn't "work." What needed to happen, though, is not mysterious. It's just a bit more complicated than she had initially thought. It's not unique, but it is commendable that she could ask for help. As with any new skill—say, dancing—some instruction may be necessary to present the steps, followed by practice.

Step One (asking and listening) would require Margo to quiet herself, to put her own frustrations, old injuries, and preconceived notions about what she'd done and intended aside for the time being. Beginning an apology with receptivity would call upon her to be brave in the face of potential discomfort. This person who is more comfortable with action and certainty would have to be open to learning from her friend. Although recognized for his boldness, British prime minister Winston Churchill is known to have said, "Courage is what it takes to stand up and speak; courage is also what it takes to sit down and listen."[17]

Margo asked Annie if she'd be willing to come into my office, so they could talk about what happened. Right away, Annie said yes.

The two arrived separately at my office and did not embrace. Although Annie greeted me warmly, she initially kept her eyes away from Margo. She was dressed in softer, more casual clothes than Margo's professional garb and was not wearing makeup, but nonetheless, the two of them sat in my red chairs in mirror postures, both crossing their legs the same way and leaning toward the other a bit.

Step One: Don't Just Do Something; Stand There

I introduced the idea that Margo wanted to ask Annie a question. Annie tilted her head and listened as Margo spoke the words she'd discussed with me: **"I'm not sure I really get what it was like for you when I cut off contact. Would you be willing to tell me about it?"**

In response, Annie looked at her old friend for the first time and began slowly: "It was just so sudden. Suddenly I couldn't even talk to you or write to you." She paused. "It was as if you died." Margo sighed but continued to listen. Annie went on, "It was terrible to lose you. And I was completely helpless to do anything about it."

Often, would-be apologizers interrupt or short-circuit this step with defensive maneuvers, attempts to justify themselves or diminish the other's complaint. You might say things like: "It wasn't as bad as you're saying." "Why are you bringing that up now / again / like that?" "I was only doing what I thought you wanted." It's especially hard to stay silent when someone characterizes your actions in ways that seem unfair or inaccurate. Nonetheless, during this step, you are not to mention your own reasons, not to mount arguments, and especially not to "counterattack."

You may ask clarifying questions if they help the other person tell her or his story, but in general this is a circumstance in which saying and doing less is better. You may feel compelled to "fix" the problem before it's fully expressed. ("We can return it and get you the right one." "Okay, I'll take the car in and pay for the repair." "You don't have to keep that appointment if you don't want to.") Fixing something specific, giving someone what you think they need, can feel terrific. But it's denying the other person a chance to speak their full truth and be heard. Inquiry requires that you give up that powerful and satisfying fix-it role and adopt a humbler posture, something like the Buddhist "beginner's mind." In couples therapy, as in broader American culture, a common piece of advice is, "Don't just do something; stand there" (attributed to those ranging from Dwight Eisenhower to the White Rabbit in Disney's *Alice in Wonderland*). That is to say, stay present. Listen.

It's natural to feel defensive when hearing about how our actions hurt a friend or loved one. That's why I encourage the person who's been hurt to use language that is as neutral as possible and employ the familiar practice of making "I" statements.

In this case, Annie didn't accuse her friend or use blaming language. Nonetheless, Margo couldn't entirely avoid defensiveness. She crossed her arms over her chest and began to compare their injuries, as if her own hurt justified her hurting Annie. "You and Sandra made me feel terrible, too, you know."

To her credit, Margo caught herself and stopped. She looked at me. I remained silent. On her own, she dropped her blocked posture and said, "Never mind. Can you continue?" Once she recommitted herself to understanding Annie, she found that she could better listen to her story.

Annie cried softly as she said, "When you broke contact, it was so much like my family rejecting me. I know it's not the same, but it felt like you abandoned me completely." As happens in almost all the relationships I've witnessed, when Margo really heard her loved one's pain, deep empathy and genuine regret followed. For Annie, the chance to be heard was particularly powerful, since Margo had shut her off months ago. Their relationship could begin to heal. This is where a loving expression of care becomes part of Step Two, as you will see.

HOW STEP ONE OFTEN COMES UP

The way the apology between these friends began is not at all unusual: Margo was blindsided by Annie's reaction. She had not considered the hurt she'd caused. Remember, we all can be clueless. Because we miss the negative effects we have on other people, we're naturally less likely to initiate an apology. So if you're waiting for someone to make an apology to you, bear in mind that they may be unaware of having harmed you. In Chapter 2, for example, Rolland focused exclusively on how his brother had hurt him, not aware of any way he may have hurt his brother.

The most common Step One opportunity arises when someone tells you you've hurt them or had an unwanted impact on them. That's a very good time to override your defensiveness—no easy feat—and ask for more information. Sometimes it takes time and more than one try for you to be open to facing the hurt you've caused. That's what happened when Jackie first approached her sister Serena.

Recently I had an opportunity to observe myself in just such a moment. I did not handle it well. On the phone last month, my brother told me that he'd been avoiding talking with me about his son Charlie because of something very hurtful I'd said last spring. Charlie had been going through a custody battle, a painful legal process that could have have ended with his children living with their mother. Because I'd been a guardian ad litem (a court-appointed advocate for a child's best interests in a disputed family court case) in Massachusetts, my brother had asked me for recommendations regarding what they could do. I'd previously learned to avoid giving him advice because he'd long ago told me that he didn't want me to. But that time he'd insisted and I'd given in. I made two recommendations.

Then, last month, when he told me on the phone that I'd been hurtful, he seemed to think (mistakenly) that I'd told him the children would be better off with their mother. I hadn't said anything close to that and hadn't thought that at all. My first reaction to my brother's accusation was to lose my temper. I was immediately furious that he was distorting what I'd said and that he'd been avoiding me as a result—not to mention that he'd led me into giving opinions in the first place.

I did not take a deep breath and consider the hurt he was telling me about. I ended the conversation angrily. We followed that aborted conversation with a lengthy text exchange that held further, mutual accusations. I spent the next few days steaming about his less-desirable characteristics. I composed (but didn't send) furious messages. Eventually I grew tired of feeling so critical and defensive. I tried to find compassion for him, but it was harder to remember that I'd had a role in that last phone conversation, too.

Here I am, writing a book about apologies and I blew Step One, big-time. I tell this story because I should know better, but my defensiveness and anger got the better of me. My brother was wrong about what I'd said and I could definitely find aspects of his actions to criticize, but that wasn't going to get me reconnected to him. Because I want a relationship with him, I had to reach out and ask him to tell me about how he'd felt hurt by what he thought I said. I had to listen first, before I could tell my side. I don't mind saying that, despite all I've learned about apologies, it was very hard for me to do.

Eventually, I told him I was sorry I'd jumped to anger so quickly and that I would like to hear what he'd been trying to tell me. He told me how hard that period had been for him and his family, and I listened. Our connection reestablished, we continued the conversation.

One common circumstance where negative feedback nets resistance rather than curiosity arises in complaints made to bosses. In many organizations, companies, and schools, the people in charge do not know what it's like for those farther down the organizational chart. Thus, they are often thrown off when they catch wind of dissatisfaction among workers. When complaints about the culture of a place or other expressions of unrest arise, the managers' resistance may be caused by their fundamental unfamiliarity with the experience of the rest of the group. Their initial surprise might become denial, stonewalling, or dismissal of employees' concerns.

Step One: Don't Just Do Something; Stand There

For example, following two racist incidents, I was asked to consult to a small college. I was charged with assessing the racial climate of the school's community. In many interviews with faculty, staff, and students, I heard about incidents of racial bias and prejudice, both subtle and obvious. When I told the leaders who'd hired me about the prevalence of such experiences, they expressed considerable doubt, even disbelief. As with individuals, organizations also often act to protect a self-image. This is not solely a public image or public relations issue but can be an identity challenge. The solution is to build in frequent, safe channels for "upward negative feedback." This is one of the places where Kim Scott's call to create a culture of honest feedback or "radical candor" is fitting.[18]

In addition, because women are more likely to internalize negative feedback than men, Suzanne Bates, an executive coach in suburban Boston, recommends that women in particular should practice receiving it at work. They should ask for frequent feedback and do something productive with it. The most successful executives, female or male, are those who "are the best at taking feedback, and they seek it their whole lives."[19]

These processes are the same as Step One in this chapter, in that they involve open-minded gathering of information—often stressful or negative—for the purpose of accurate understanding and the opportunity to make things better. As such, seeking feedback contributes to the establishment of psychological safety, in which people can share and face difficult information with one another.

HOW LONG DOES IT TAKE?

Many hurts, especially old ones, take more than one brief conversation to express and understand. How long it takes isn't universal or predictable, which can be frustrating to the apologizer who wants to move on. But you have to have the whole conversation. If you remember that this process is not about the endgame of absolution, you will understand that it takes time, attention, and patience not only to restore a relationship, but also to make it stronger than it was. Adrienne Maree Brown, a social justice activist who writes about how to make conflict transformational rather than destructive, recommends we take more time to address hurt or conflict, much more time than our reactive customs usually allow. "Real time is slower than social media time, where everything feels urgent. Real time often includes periods of silence, reflection, growth, space, self-forgiveness, processing with loved ones, rest, and responsibility."[20]

After major injuries, such as betrayals or unfaithfulness, hearing the whole experience of the hurt person can take a relatively long time. Oftentimes, before Step One is complete, some parts of the story must be heard more than once. Emotions have their own idiosyncratic arcs, which have to be honored. In his poem "Crying," Galway Kinnell advises the reader to cry and cry until all the tears are cried. He writes, "Happiness [hides] in the last tear."[21] Change and relief won't come until the hurt person is ready to move on.

Jonny and Sarah, both red-eyed and weary-looking, began their consultation with uncomfortable silences and difficulty completing sentences. In their early thirties, they arrived in my office wearing jeans, sweaters, and snow boots. A few years earlier, they'd fallen in love, an unlikely pair from divergent cultural and religious backgrounds. They'd dated steadily for only a few months and, since then, had been separated off and on due to their graduate school and early career training. They'd worked hard to stay connected during long periods apart. Now as they approached the end of their geographical separation, they had been looking forward to the next stage of their relationship. For the first time in a long while, they'd be in the same city for an extended period. They'd planned to look for a place to live together.

Step One: Don't Just Do Something; Stand There

However, three weeks earlier, Jonny had come across Sarah's communications with an ex-boyfriend—someone Jonny had heard of but not thought much about—in which they planned to get together during a professional trip. As he'd scrolled down, he'd found that previous messages had progressed from nostalgic flirtation and curiosity to explicitly sexual comments. That day, Jonny had boxed up all Sarah's belongings from his apartment and left them outside his door. He'd piled all their shared camping equipment next to her personal effects and texted her to come get them.

Immediately, she'd stopped communications with the former boyfriend and told Jonny she was extremely sorry. In the days since, they'd had several emotional scenes in which Jonny had veered from never wanting to talk to her again to yelling at her or crying about her "horrible" actions. Sarah had begged him to forgive her and had sunk into a dark place of self-recrimination and hopelessness. They kept their separate apartments.

Although their plans had all blown up and the painful pieces hadn't landed yet, Sarah wanted to be sure I knew that they had a very strong bond and that they both had expected to get married.

"At least *I thought so* . . . before," countered Jonny, looking down. I couldn't tell if he was more angry or sad.

Sarah leaned toward him, grabbing the arms of her chair tightly for balance. "Everything we've had together isn't suddenly not true. We've had so many sweet times over the years." He avoided her gaze. She turned to me. "What happened doesn't change the past!"

"No," I agreed, "but it can definitely make us question what we thought was true."

"Exactly!" Jonny shot out. "You know how much I loved those times when it was just the two of us in the middle of nowhere. Now I don't know if I can trust anything about you. Or about us."

"Right." I stepped in to interrupt angry recriminations at this point. "Things between you have clearly reached a terribly hard impasse. I understand from talking to you both by phone that you nonetheless want to try to get through this together. Is that right?"

"Yes," Sarah spoke quickly. "Like I told you, I'm ashamed and upset that I screwed everything up and hurt him so badly. Jonny is the person I want to be with."

Jonny didn't respond right away, shaking his head and taking a deep breath. "I go back and forth. I've loved her for such a long time, but I can't believe she would do this to me. She's not the person I thought she was." After another silence, he continued, "I do want to get to the other side of this crap with her. I wish we could go back to— I don't know—a night on a mountain trail. I just can't imagine how we could get there again."

I then explained, "I asked about your goals because repairing this hurt will be challenging. We can't know yet whether you two will end up together, but I do know that you can take steps to heal from this awful hurt."

In our next meeting, Jonny began to say, "How can I ever trust you—" but Sarah started to weep.

Through her tears, she broke in: "I've told you so many times I'm sorry!"

Despite Sarah's misery, I advised them that she still needed to hear more about Jonny's hurt. Her upset, though genuine, had the potential to interfere with his chance to talk and her ability to listen. Remember, Step One is not a demand for forgiveness. It's not about the apologizer's regrets or guilt.

For Sarah and Jonny, her patience became the steady keel that got them through the storm she caused by her breach of trust. During the ensuing months, they were not really "together," though they were never far from each other's mind. They talked frequently and spent some time together. It was a strange, fluid situation for them. For the first time in years, neither of them went hiking or camping, something they'd done together frequently. A few times, Jonny instituted periods when he didn't see Sarah at all. During those periods, she was plagued by brutal guilt and loneliness. She also dealt with painful embarrassment that his family knew about her errant behavior and the hurt she'd caused. Without involving him much, she tried to face her shame and guilt.

For his part, Jonny always believed her regret to be sincere and hoped that he would want to be with her again, but he wasn't ready. Timing is a crucial, often unrecognized feature of effective relationship repair—not only how long it takes, but how ready you are to make or accept an apology. In this sense, healing from a relationship breach is like recovering from a physical injury. If you're in too much pain, you can't be curious and open. If your injury is very fresh, you can't do much in physical therapy at first. Be patient, but keep moving.

After the first few sessions, we met only periodically and not always together. Jonny had to go through a process not unlike grief, in which he mourned the loss of his previous, innocent trust in Sarah. That disappointment initially rocked him and reawakened an earlier sense of betrayal he'd encountered with his first, adolescent love. He told Sarah about how preoccupied he was at times with imagining her being with the other guy.

Coaching for Sarah through the spring and summer included promoting self-care and helping her find her personal balance. This helped her to stand steadily by while her boyfriend continued to tell her about his hurt and to work his way through his mistrust. In their case, the "Don't just do something; stand there" maxim required Sarah to "stand there for a long time."

Many people get stuck here, their shame spiraling inward and interfering with anything productive. Crucially, Sarah became curious about herself instead. In individual therapy, she examined the motivations for her actions, meanings that had been opaque to her. Not only did she learn to understand this awful episode, but she also came to recognize other patterns in her warm interpersonal style. She examined her fears of deepening her commitment to Jonny and reconfirmed that he was the person she wanted to be with. She began to forgive herself.

Bear in mind, then, although the needs of the hurt person take precedence, the apologizer also requires care. An extended Step One can tax your patience and self-esteem. If repairing the relationship in question is deeply important to you, as it was to Sarah, you may need to build up your resilience for a longer haul than you anticipated. Self-compassion can be crucially helpful in order to sustain such courage and openness. It is remarkably hard work. Supportive friends, self-examination—which Sarah did in psychotherapy—and spiritual practices helped her center and calm herself. Specific strategies and resources can include meditation, mindfulness, and prayer, as well as yoga, qigong, tai chi, and exercise.

As she developed stronger internal balance, Sarah trusted herself more to listen and wait. Meanwhile, Jonny found that he valued her many wonderful traits, including her genuine care through this hard time. Ultimately, he had to learn what she was like, really, in all her human complexity, replacing his early, idealized view of her.

They both were relieved and happy when Jonny wanted to spend regular time together again. Eventually, in my office, they decided they were ready to get out their tent and camping stove and head together to the nearby White Mountains. On their return, they told me that they'd had what they called a "mountain moment" together: High in the mountains, under the expansive sky, they were able to have a deep and honest discussion about what really mattered to them and what they meant to each other. They deeply appreciated each other and found that they were both proud of how they'd handled the previous months. Sharing wide-open space helped them find clarity about what they valued most.

This couple got through a very hard time partly because they were able to stay clear about their goal. They both wanted to build a trustworthy, loving relationship with the other. During their months mostly apart, Sarah had begun to engage in the other apology steps, but also returned to Step One again and again until Jonny had told his story enough.

The question "What is enough?" arises in many extended Step One efforts. The process can wear you down. Partners ask, "Shouldn't she be past it by now?" Or "Will I ever be out of the doghouse?" Understandably, one person or the other may feel tempted to cut their losses. In Chapter 10, we will consider when an apology process isn't working or shouldn't be continued. But in my experience, couples can get through almost anything if they stay the course with patience, perseverance, and compassion. Pay attention to loving intentions and small moments of mutual learning. They are not as exciting as dramatic change, nor as conclusive as fairy-tale happy endings, but if you're building something to last, it takes time and careful work to reassemble.

By the time winter settled back into Boston, Sarah and Jonny had found a level of comfort and happiness with each other that they described as "much stronger" than they'd felt before their problem had arisen. Theirs had been a new connection when they began their long-distance relationship. Now they knew each other—and themselves— much better. They approached the future together with well-grounded optimism. This strengthening is a version of what Esther Perel, the well-known marital therapist and writer, has observed as some couples work through an actual affair. Even if a couple has been together for decades, a thorough repair process creates greater mutual knowledge, empathy, and intimacy. (In Chapter 8, we'll spell out an apology's aftereffects further.)

With time, patience, and care, Sarah was able to listen to Jonny and regain his trust. But too many people discourage their partners from expressing hurt fully.

NOT LISTENING PREVENTS HEALING

Here's a story I often hear: Renee complains to her partner, Jordan, that he's let her down by failing to follow through on something. It could've been a small thing, like getting the oil changed in the car, or a large one, like forgetting to show up for something really important. In this couple, Jordan's habitual response to whatever problem Renee raises is to become caught up in his own awful feelings. He may leave the room or slam a door. Later he acts withdrawn or down and says things like, "I guess I screwed up once again." He becomes overwhelmed with contrition or its more insidious relative, shame, and his statements become more extreme: "I can never do anything right," "I'm just a terrible husband," or "You probably don't really want to be with me." As she is forced to reckon with (or tend to) his unhappiness, Renee's original concern falls by the wayside. As a result, she doesn't have the satisfaction of being heard fully by her partner, much less having the problem addressed and repaired.

This dynamic makes Renee reluctant to bring up any future hurts. She doesn't want to cause Jordan so much pain and, increasingly, she lacks faith that she will be free to speak, much less that the problem will be solved. Unresolved conflicts like these tend to stay around.

This is the same pattern we heard about from Lisa Earle McLeod, sales leadership expert for Forbes.com. Failing to address and resolve conflict in a business setting keeps employees stuck in the same problem.[22] If you can't face a conflict together, you have no chance to change the way anyone involved—including yourself— views it. You can't reach a new agreement, nor can you change something you don't like.

Partners like Jordan might have other apology skills, but they don't reach the later apology steps because they get stuck at Step One. They don't listen and learn about their partners' experiences. These couples become burdened by chronic, unspoken resentment. For Renee, frustration grows because, due to Jordan's big, personalized reaction, she doesn't have a forum to express herself or ask for relatively small course adjustments. For his part, unless Jordan challenges his quick-trigger emotional responses, he won't learn how to listen to her. As things are, he has very little idea about the real effect he's having on her. This pattern can lead to escalating anger and what look like periodic overreactions by Renee, which create more conflict and can lead them into therapy. More dangerous to the relationship are hopelessness and distance, which often lead to therapy only after it's too late.

But it is possible to learn to change these patterns. For example, whether or not they come to therapy, each member of the couple can change their customary responses. By engaging in a discipline like stress management or mindfulness training, Jordan can learn to slow down his reactivity. Then he'll be able to listen better to Renee's words and to respond to just her message, not to his worried thoughts about himself. As with any other behavioral change, Jordan can train himself to take a moment to breathe before he says or does anything in response to her. If he's curious about the fears or self-doubts underlying his emotional reactions, he can explore them in therapy or elsewhere.

For her part, Renee can learn to hold on to the initial point she's trying to make and, if it doesn't get across to him at first, to try again. Rather than giving up, she can introduce a question about when might be a good time to discuss it. Her challenge is to remember that her hurt or disappointment matters and that making her feelings clear to Jordan is not a bad thing for their relationship; it's valuable. This is an example of the truism "Clarity is kindness." This type of couple will have a much better outcome if she can hold him accountable, despite his reactions, and he can learn to focus on his impact on her. In order to challenge their unfortunate shared habit, they may have to go back and air earlier hurts—what sometimes seems like going over ancient history—to rework interactions that were never completed in the past.

A Good Apology

WHEN *NOT* TO "JUST STAND THERE"

What if the other person isn't aware of harm you've done to them? What if you've done something like what Sarah did (when she approached infidelity), but your partner didn't find out? Or, as people mention in apology workshops, what if you regret a pattern of thoughtlessness or taking for granted—something your partner may not have overtly noticed? If you're committed to making this kind of wrong right, you have to enter the dance with a different step. You probably will begin with Step Two, which involves a statement of regret and responsibility. Following that, you can invite your partner to respond to your statement and express how they feel about what you've described—Step One—at which point you shift to being receptive. During this step of the process, you will follow rather than lead.

Sometimes, even when known harm has occurred, it isn't possible or a good idea to engage with the person who's been affected by your actions. If it would definitely cause further harm, you mustn't. If you are worried about it, search for a way to invite the conversation that doesn't awaken hurt. For example, **"I wonder if you would like to talk with me about what happened between us a long time ago [or at a specific time or circumstance]. If not, it's completely your choice and I understand. If you are interested, I'd like to tell you about some regrets I have."**
If listening to the hurt person is not an option, either because they're not available or because it would cause additional harm, asking other people familiar with the circumstance or with the victim may help. Perhaps they could teach you what you need to know—again, unless it's intrusive or painful, which would constitute another harm. When it's not possible to pursue information about the actual person involved, sometimes vicarious inquiry is worthwhile; that is, other people who've been hurt like the original person may be willing to teach

you, the one who's done harm. In a program operated by Mothers Against Drunk Driving, people who've been affected by an impaired driver sit on Victim Impact Panels, which offenders attend.[23] Survivors and family members of victims do not speak to the particular offenders responsible for the harm they've experienced, but many can (and want to) tell their stories of injury and loss. Listening to stories about incidents other than their own offenses can help perpetrators feel more empathy than they may have previously felt for their own victims. This listening and learning can lead offenders to accept more responsibility for the harm they caused.

Regardless of whatever it takes for you to hear and absorb an injured person's story, once you've been able to, you've begun a good apology. The next steps will also require patience, humility, and courage—those things you've already been practicing. But as you've moved through Step One, you've created a sense of momentum. Healing has already begun.

Remember that no one should be defined by the worst of their mistakes. What you do next will influence your future and your relationship's future more powerfully than anything you've already done.

PRACTICE SCRIPTS FOR STEP ONE

- "I thought I knew what happened, but apparently I'm missing something. Would you fill me in, please?"

- "I said I was sorry for what I did, but it seems like there's something else I don't get."

- "I've got a pretty good idea of what's going on, but I think there might be more I should know about how what I did affected you."

- "Obviously I touched a raw nerve, and I want to know more about it so I don't do it again."

- "Look, something I did hit you in a really bad way and I truly want to understand what happened."

- "I want to understand what's going on. Please tell me all about it."

- "I want to understand. I'll do my best just to listen."

- "Thank you for bringing up how I affected you. I want to hear about it."

CHAPTER 5

Step Two: Say It and Mean It

In Step Two, you show that you understand the way(s) the other person has been hurt and that you care about it. This is when you express your empathy. You also hold yourself accountable for any actions that have contributed to the negative experience of the other.

Monique couldn't bear to hear Desmond say it. She visibly flinched when he accused her of letting him down the previous weekend. At a holiday event, her children from her previous marriage (ages six to eleven) had "rudely" ignored him, barely spoken to him. In my office, Monique's lips pressed together and her face flushed. She fumed, no longer focused on what Desmond was saying. As he went on to express his frustration with her and the family, even divulging that at times he had felt tempted to leave their three-year marriage, she began to break into his speech with counterpoint and argument. She became heated in her defense of the children's decency and manners. She insisted, "Nobody meant to hurt your feelings, Desmond," "I'm not a cold person," and "It's not my fault you got upset!"

When we discuss blame, we have the basis for a debate, which suits a legal proceeding just fine but works in the wrong direction in a relationship. As we learned in the previous chapter, the first step in an apology is when a person learns about someone else's experience of hurt, regardless of who's at fault. Most of us dread being singled out as the one to blame for a problem, to be wrong or "bad," which we fear will result if we engage in a reckoning process like an apology.

In our session, I recommended that Monique hold her reactions for the moment. I suggested, "Try to hear Desmond's description of what happened from his point of view, not in terms of who was or wasn't at fault for it." At first, she literally rolled her eyes—resistant in the same way most of us are. But—also like many of us—Monique could hold herself in check, at least for a little while. A little while may be long enough to cool your ire and allow you to hear the other person.

I asked Desmond to describe to Monique only how he felt—not who he thought was to blame, but just focusing on his own experience. Desmond described one frustrating occasion after another when he tried to join in. He slipped a bit: "Your kids ignored what I said, like they always do."

I spoke up before either of them could continue. "For now, Desmond, see if you can focus—"

"On telling Monique how I felt. I know." He smiled nervously at his wife. "Slow learner."

I wanted to normalize his limitation. "We all are slow at learning this pattern. Changing habits isn't easy."

Monique gave him a slight nod back.

Desmond exhaled. "Anyway, the main thing is I felt left out of things and like I didn't belong." He paused and gazed directly at her. "That's a feeling I've always hated."

In most couples I've known, compassion naturally follows a revelation of the other's suffering, even when they've been sparring about its cause. When Monique really heard her husband, she no longer needed to resist his basic message.

Empathy followed. "I do feel bad that you spent what was supposed to be a fun time feeling left out. **I'm sorry I didn't realize what was going on. I completely missed how upsetting this was.**"

She reached across to take his hand. They both seemed relieved as they sat in silence for a moment.

Note that Monique hadn't accepted blame for his bad feelings. Step Two, to state one's regret, is much easier once our defenses have lowered. But taking responsibility for repair doesn't always mean accepting blame. Monique wanted to restore their relationship balance and to help her partner feel better, so she was motivated to examine her own contributions to the situation. In all honesty, though, she didn't see that her immediate behavior had caused her husband's problem at the party. But she did take responsibility for failing to pick up on the children's behavior or his reactions.

Desmond told her, "I appreciate that, sweetie, but..." He grimaced as he turned to me and said, "I hate to say this, but I think there's more we need to talk about, bigger things."

Although the information wasn't welcome, this time Monique's walls didn't go so far up. "Uh-oh!" She kept hold of his hand. "Well, this is probably the time to say it."

Speaking directly to her, he said, "I know you've heard this before, and I don't want to make you feel bad, but how the kids treat me is only one of a bunch of things you promised that have turned out to be anything but true."

I asked, "Want to clarify what they are?"

"She knows. We've been over it all before. How we spend money, weekends we don't go away together, visits with our families [of origin], and"—his voice broke a little bit—"the kind of family we'd be."

"That's a collection of really important things. Is there one that's especially important?"

"I guess so." He turned to her. "Before we got married, you talked a lot about how we would parent together and be a team, how we'd be a close, warm family. I didn't have any of that growing up and I really wanted us to have it together, Monique. I know we can't control how people feel, but it doesn't seem like we've even tried." He paused. "I don't know how to tell you how disappointing this whole thing is."

"'Whole thing'?" I asked.

"Our whole—our life together isn't what I thought it would be."

"Marriage rarely unfolds exactly as we expect—" I began, until Monique broke in.

"But he's right! I *did* promise all those things and lots of them *haven't* happened. I knew he didn't like it, but I thought we were doing okay, anyway."

Desmond shrugged and looked away. They were no longer holding hands.

"Okay, so I guess we're not." She sat for a couple of minutes. Again, the blame question came up: "This isn't all my fault. Lots of things changed that I had nothing to do with. You know that, D." She spoke at some length, giving examples of her challenges, including her work demands and the kids' sports schedules. To me, she continued: "I never would do anything to hurt him. Do *you* think it's my fault?"

"It sounds like you've made some mistakes that have hurt Desmond."

She turned to him. "Is it too late? Have you given up?"

"Well, that's why I wanted to come see Molly. I really want things to be different if they can be."

She looked back and forth from him to me, as realization of the seriousness of his dissatisfaction seemed to sink in.

* * *

This is the kind of moment when I'm tempted to be reassuring, to help a patient feel better about what she's done and more hopeful about the relationship. As Avi Klein, the psychotherapist mentioned in Chapter 1, wrote, it's much harder to do the genuinely therapeutic thing and hold people accountable, to help them face the consequences of what they've done.[1]

I said, "Let's look at the things you *can* take responsibility for. It seems like there's more than one kind of problem between you two, important hurts that need mending. First of all, Monique, is it possible that you haven't paid enough attention to the promises you didn't keep, like you haven't really paid attention to your husband's recent unhappiness? Is it at all like the kids at the party, where you don't really notice—even after he tells you?"

"I said I was sorry that I didn't notice!"

A pause, while she caught her breath. "Okay, okay." To her credit, Monique stopped defending herself and spoke directly to him, **"Desmond, I guess I haven't really taken *a lot* of your reactions seriously enough, which isn't fair to you. I'm sorry."**

His eyes reddened as she spoke, but he just nodded.

"That's a really important statement to make. Nice work." But I kept her feet to the fire, reminding her gently, "How about the broken promises?"

Monique responded, "I've stopped arguing about that. What else am I supposed to do?"

"How do you want to fix it?"

Monique said, "Damn, I don't know," but she had already shown that she could begin with a good statement of apology.

"Let's start with telling him how you feel about not keeping your promise to work together as parents."

She took time to think through what she wanted to say. **"I'm incredibly sorry I just let my promises go, when they turned out to be too hard and we were so busy. I didn't even talk to**

you about how we could make things better for our family. You mean the world to me, D, and I guess I haven't shown you that very well."

They both teared up, then stood and embraced.

Monique hadn't apologized for all the promises she hadn't followed through on, some of which may not have ever been possible to keep. What she did do was take responsibility for *not dealing with* her broken promises, for failing to acknowledge them, and for not noticing the effect those lapses had on her partner. In order to change the situation going forward, Desmond and Monique still needed to figure out how to address challenging family dynamics and the reasons the problematic patterns developed—but they could do that only once they had begun to face the disappointments and hurt that had been souring their relationship (Step One) and Monique had made it clear that she regretted how her actions and failure to act affected her husband (Step Two).

In Step Two, you take responsibility for the impact you had on the other person, even if you didn't intend to hurt them.

Initially Monique had been resistant, because she didn't want to be blamed for Desmond's bad feelings. But after she really understood her husband's experience of exclusion at the party, she could consider how she'd contributed to his unhappiness. Monique didn't feel like she caused it, but she was able to offer a solid statement of remorse for missing Desmond's emotional state. Similarly, she could address the effects of her failure to deal with her promises that hadn't come true.

It can be hard to accept, but when you begin a real apology, nothing about you (the apologizer)—your motives, your character, your justification—is relevant. As I worked with Margo, the woman from Chapter 4 who wanted to repair her relationship with her friend Annie, she realized that, while she had initially approached the second step, she had not undertaken it thoroughly enough. Once she'd gained a greater understanding of how her avoidance of conflict had hurt Annie, Margo's new statement to her was personal and direct: **"I'm really sorry I made you feel so much pain from earlier in your life. I want to be a supportive person for you, not a harming one. I wish I'd been able to see your point of view, instead of focusing only on mine."** It was a very different statement from her first, partial apology, when she'd emailed a quick "I'm sorry, but" statement, which was more about her own upset than the hurt she'd caused Annie.

You might mistakenly focus on yourself for any number of other reasons. Perhaps you can't see the other person's experience or perhaps you want to avoid being held accountable. The excellent blog *Sorry-Watch* parses the value of public apologies with an (excuse the expression) unapologetically critical eye. For example, Mark Zuckerberg's 2018 appearance before Congress about Facebook's failure to protect users' data included a rejection of responsibility with the statement "That's not who we are." This comment, although common, is a poor response for a few reasons. One is that, as *SorryWatch* frequently points out, the would-be apologizer erred by focusing on himself, rather than his effect on the other person(s) and taking responsibility for it.[2] Furthermore, "that" actually *is* "who they are" or this problem wouldn't have come up. It probably isn't who they want to be or wish they were or what they want to stand for in the world—all of which would be better statements. You evade responsibility when you deny the fact of your error.

As I've pointed out, many people do not believe they are at fault for a problem, so they don't want to address the reaction another person has. We don't like the idea that we caused pain because we don't want to think of ourselves as "the kind of person" who hurts others. It's understandable to want to preserve a self-concept as a good, nice person, but the two are not contradictory: The kind of person who causes pain, often by mistake, is *every kind of person*. Relationships are like a contact sport: We frequently bang and bruise one another, often without meaning to cause harm. If we want to participate fully, we need to develop the skills to recover from the inevitable hurts and get back in the game—hopefully together.

David and Jake, middle-aged now, had been best friends since high school. David had spent countless hours at Jake's house and had built a warm relationship with Jake's parents, especially his usually gruff and irritable father, Harry. When Harry decided to sell the family home five years after his wife's death, the two friends helped him sort belongings. For thirty years, they'd shared a decidedly goofy sense of humor, riffing at length on each other's questionable puns. As they boxed treasured family things and Jake set aside mementos for his children, they exercised their trademark comedy throughout the day. A few weeks later, David saw a tweet from Jake's sister Melanie that accused him of disrespecting her (and Jake's) dead mother. She said she'd heard from her aunt that his "juvenile" and "insensitive" behavior had upset Harry.

In Jake's family, as in many families and other groups, people use an indirect route to communicate problematic feelings. You may have been surprised by just such a she-told-somebody-who-told-somebody-else message at some point and wondered how to handle it. David's first reaction was anger at Melanie, who was known as the family member who stirred up and exaggerated trouble. He thought everyone in Jake's family should know by now that he would never deliberately hurt Harry or insult his wife and that his habit of silliness with Jake was harmless.

We've seen how tempting it is to confuse our intentions, particularly our conscious, fully aware intentions, with the effects of our actions, but they are somewhat independent of each other. In their studies of human cognition, Princeton University researchers Daniel Ames and Susan Fiske found that your perceptions of intent influence your perceptions of impact. In other words, if you believe someone's harmful actions are inadvertent mistakes, you tend to minimize their cost to others. You inaccurately estimate: If the intent wasn't bad, the impact can't be so big.[3] In fact, accidental hurt can be very big.

A rush of anger at someone for feedback or an accusation is understandable. (You might remember my unfortunate response to my brother.) If it's allowed to rule your response, it can prevent you from learning about your effect on someone. As the Buddhist teacher and writer Pema Chodron wrote, both the suppression of anger and the acting out of it make things worse. She recommends "patience: wait, experience the anger and investigate its nature."[4] My Buddhist friends talk about "surfing the urge," which means noticing your inclination to act and freeing yourself from taking action. As you continue to notice, you can learn a lot.

In response to Melanie's tweet, David was tempted to fire off a hostile tweet of his own. Fortunately, he held back. As he thought about the situation for the next couple of days, he felt bad that Harry might have been hurt or felt insulted by him. He also considered what leaving the old house probably meant to Harry—and Melanie and Jake, for that matter. A lot of sad feelings had probably come up for the whole family. Although he hadn't intended any disrespect, he understood how the day could have made family members more vulnerable or on edge. He decided to apologize to Harry directly.

He called Harry, asked if he had a minute, and told him, **"I understand I didn't show proper respect last month when I was goofing around at the house. I'm really sorry my humor made a hard day harder for you."**

Harry cleared his throat and took a moment to reply. Then he told him, "Don't worry about it. It's what I expect from you two knuckleheads"—which had been his familiar term for them in high school.

I include this story because David's responsibility taking is such a lovely example of Step Two. After the initial exchange, he then inquired into Harry's experience (Step One). Harry seemed to appreciate the question and responded warmly. He admitted that he'd been annoyed by the horseplay. But, moreover, he went on to share with David how painful it had been to leave the house, unrelated to David's and Jake's actions. It was a more personal revelation than had ever passed between them. Their relationship had deepened.

David could have made any number of cases in his defense: that he hadn't done anything wrong, that he had only benign intentions, that Melanie was frequently off base, that neither she nor her aunt were present so they didn't know what they were talking about, that Jake was equally at fault for any harm, that Harry should know him better than to be hurt by him. But he didn't. David didn't like hearing that his actions may have hurt someone he cared about, but his priority was making sure that his relationship with Harry hadn't been damaged—regardless of whether or not Melanie had blown things out of proportion. He made a proactive, direct apology to the person he inadvertently hurt. Not surprisingly, it worked—in the sense that balance and comfort were reestablished between David and Harry—and they actually became closer.

Between people, the ideal outcome is not simply justice, but to create connection and greater mutual understanding. That's what relationship repair is all about.

But, as we saw in Chapter 2, it isn't what normal brain functioning is all about. We are cognitively and perceptually biased to believe we are right, despite extensive evidence that we are often wrong. Frequently, we fail to consider others' perspectives, we don't see our mistakes or the negative effects we have, and we view the world from our own points of view.

On his own, David took crucial time to think about the feedback he'd gotten on Twitter. With great sensitivity, he realized that he had missed an important element of the house-closing situation. Couples therapy routinely requires a similar reset of perception. For example, because she listened to her husband, Monique saw that she'd been wearing blinders about his experience. Then, in their own ways, Monique and David each took steps to make things right. If you take with you only one message from this book, I hope it will be the perpetual need to remember that what you know is never the whole story. Bear in mind what Kathryn Schulz, the wrongology expert, recommends: Remember to attend to counterevidence.[5]

GUIDELINES FOR STEP TWO

Step Two, the statement of regret and responsibility, is what most people think of when they hear the word "apology." It's of central importance for sure but usually isn't the whole story. In this section, you'll find several guidelines for making good apology statements. But first I want to point out a few important truths:

- This impulse to make things right with another person is one of the most basic human tendencies.
- There are no magic words, but the words you need already reside within you. (Although many of us need guidance about how to apologize, you can make your Step Two messages to important people, like Monique, David, and Margo did, without anyone telling you what to say.)
- What lies in your heart, that is, your sincere concern about the hurt someone else experienced and your remorse about having caused it, is far more important than the technique you use to express it. Listen to your heart on this. (The biggest reason to engage your mind is to get past your resistances, so you can *get* to Step Two.)

* * *

That said, here are elements of an effective Step Two:

Take responsibility for restoring trust. In order to take personal responsibility for fixing something that's gone awry, you have to handle critical details like initiating conversation with the other person. In a workplace, this can mean setting up a scheduled appointment and making sure the other knows you want to apologize, "clear the air," "clarify misunderstandings," or "get back on good footing together." If you're heading into a conversation that may become contentious, business consultant Judith Glaser recommends that you "start by outlining rules of engagement" (the purpose of the conversation, the length of the meeting, even guidelines for respectful communication, if needed), so everyone knows what to expect.[6]

In a personal relationship, it's good to give the other person some say over the circumstances of the conversation. Bad timing accounts for many failed communication attempts. Marriage therapists Patricia Love and Steven Stosny suggest that you let the other know you intend to mend the breach between you. If the other person isn't ready or doesn't reciprocate, sometimes a wordless gesture toward reconnection, like a hand on the shoulder, is the only first step you can take in the beginning.[7]

Even if you begin with sincerity and care, an apology doesn't always go quickly. Richard Boothman, of the Michigan medical apology movement, tells a story that illustrates the persistence that is sometimes required. A patient was partially blinded by a surgical error. In both the first and second meetings scheduled for the family to discuss what happened with the surgeon and staff, the injured patient's wife left the room immediately because she was too upset. The hospital team kept showing up because they were committed to restoring trust if they could. On the third attempt, she was able to stay and both sides spoke. Mr. Boothman describes a "transformational moment" when they finally heard each other.[8] What made the difference was the persistence and patience of the medical team. They were committed to helping this family heal and knew that the woman's inability to talk to them the first few times did not mean that the conversation had to be over. That's similar to the responsibility you can take for the apologies you need to make in your life.

Talk directly to the person affected. In the story described earlier, David was told by a third party that his friend's dad had been hurt by his actions. He countered the family style of indirect communication, went straight to the person he had hurt, and did what he could to heal their relationship.

Indirect inquiry, that is, speaking to someone else about what the hurt person felt, can be tempting. And as discussed in Chapter 4, sometimes it's your only option. Most frequently, though, this kind of communication pattern leads to a game of telephone or gossip, where information gets distorted. Worse, conveying your regrets by way of someone else seems cowardly and insincere. This kind of poor apology can do the opposite of its intended purpose: The hurt person feels confused, possibly manipulated, and ultimately worse. It's face-to-face humanity that makes the difference in a statement of empathy and responsibility.

For example, former vice president Joe Biden has told many people that he owes Anita Hill an apology for how his Senate Judiciary Committee treated her. In the 1991 confirmation hearings for Supreme Court justice Clarence Thomas, committee members harshly interrogated her about her claims of sexual harassment. Their behavior has been widely criticized as disrespectful, if not aggressive. However, over twenty-eight years, Mr. Biden hadn't even tried to deliver that apology to *her*, which had left the mistreatment unaddressed for her and raised questions about his sincerity. In Ms. Hill's home, it became a family joke: If someone knocked on the door when the Hills weren't expecting anyone, they said, "Oh, is that Joe Biden coming to apologize?"[9]

For far too long, he left the offense only indirectly addressed and the subject unsettled. When he finally did reach out to her, just as he announced his candidacy for president in the 2020 race, he made a seriously flawed attempt. He neglected to take responsibility for his own actions in the situation. What he said was that he regretted "what she endured," that he was "sorry for the way she got treated" by his colleagues.[10] That's more like the condolence or sympathy "I'm sorry" than an apology "I'm sorry." For good measure, he also failed to deliver Steps Three and Four: He did not make any attempt at restitution, and he did nothing to change the future of such harmful experiences.

Suitably, Ms. Hill did not accept his communication as a good apology.[11]

In restorative justice processes, an offender's obligation includes sending an apology letter directly to anyone affected by the offense. The first person addressed is the one who's directly harmed, of course, but the requirement can also include letters to the families of the victim and the offender, as well as to additional members of the community.

It's about the other person, not you. The essence of your Step Two statement is compassion for the hurt person, not your own redemption. Your message should be grounded in their experience. When training doctors to participate in "disclosure and apology" after medical errors, Harvard Medical School proposes several guidelines for how to talk with patients and families about difficult outcomes and "adverse events." Core relational values are transparency, respect, accountability, continuity, and kindness (TRACK), but the one over-arching rule that trumps them all is that *the needs of patients and families come first.*[12]

Emphasizing the human connection in relationship repair, social psychologists Carol Tavris and Elliot Aronson concluded from their study of self-justification in relationships that, in order to ensure success as a couple, you must put empathy for your partner above defending your own territory.[13] C. S. Lewis has made an often-quoted distinction between thinking less of yourself and thinking of yourself less, which he called "humility."

Be humble. It's underrated. An effective apology requires a combination of courage and humility—to be able both to face what could be scary and unpleasant and to be vulnerable. As we've discussed, some misinterpret the demonstration of humility to be a sign of weakness; in truth, it may be an indication of tremendous inner strength. Practicing humility requires you to be open to recognition of your limitations and to learning more. What researchers call the "quiet ego" is a similar construct, linked to a balance between the interests of self and other, as well as to self-awareness and compassion.[14]

If women are said to apologize too much—what writer Ruth Whippman recently called "the patient zero of the assertiveness movement"—many problems can be "traced back to a fundamental unwillingness among men to apologize, or even perceive that they have anything to apologize for." In contrast to the popular "lean in" advice to women, she proposed that we encourage men to "lean out," that is, exercise more "deference, humility, cooperation, and listening skills."[15]

Complicating the recommendation, the *Harvard Business Review* praises leaders who embody a seemingly paradoxical combination of traits: both fierce resolve and personal humility. Jim Collins, a high-profile business consultant and author, wrote that this "Level 5 Leadership" is a counterintuitive, even countercultural, model but is the one that can transform good companies into great ones.[16]

Most of us aren't trying to transform companies, but we are trying to make peace. Nelson Mandela is frequently quoted as saying, "Great peacemakers are all people of integrity, of honesty, but humility."

It also takes bravery and fierce resolve for you to be humble in the face of your regret or guilt. So, if you're trying to mend something between you and another person, see if you can find that balance of courage and humility. It will help you pull off Step Two.

Be accountable for what you did—or didn't do. This means full disclosure. In the realm of medical errors, that requires an accounting of what happened, who's responsible for what went wrong, why it happened, and how it could have been prevented. It requires someone saying, **"I am so sorry, we made a mistake, we are responsible"** or **"I want to apologize to you—I made a serious error, I am responsible."**[17]

After a Boston surgeon made the terrible mistake of operating on the wrong leg of his patient, he told the patient directly how deeply sorry he was. Although he took responsibility for the error, the hospital's examination of the problem discovered several errors in systems that were designed to prevent these mistakes from ever happening. The hospital, Beth Israel Deaconess Medical Center, initially allowed the surgeon to remain unnamed. But his practice reached out personally to each one of his other patients, informed them that he had been the doctor who'd made this mistake, and told them that they would be helped to find a different doctor if they understandably wanted to. Not a single one did.[18] The power of holding yourself accountable is undeniable. It makes you more trustworthy. Remember the finding that businesses that had made a mistake and corrected it were more trusted than those that hadn't made a mistake? Same thing.

As you saw, David took responsibility for his childish behavior when he apologized to Harry. Jackie's sister Serena held herself accountable both for actions Jackie knew about and for some she didn't. Without defending or denying, they both allowed the other person simply to respond and, if possible, to forgive. In your apologies, you have to say what actions (or failures to act) you're taking responsibility for and apologize for the harm you caused the other person.

When there isn't an ongoing relationship, an accountable apology still goes a long way. On *The Daily* podcast, Caitlin Flanagan told the story of how she was sexually assaulted when she was in high school. The attack had serious consequences for her mental health and was nearly lethal. However, her assailant later approached her with remorse. She described how he took full responsibility for his harmful behavior in a mature and heartfelt way. She believes his apology is the reason she hasn't felt tormented by the experience across the years, as many other survivors do.[19] His good apology helped her genuinely heal from a terrible experience.

Regardless of the seriousness of the harm, your responsible apology might help someone, too.

Mean it when you say it. If your apology doesn't seem genuine, it won't be effective. This is a moment in life when honest responsibility taking is your only real option.

A recent trend in public apologies is the use of technology to create moments of pseudo-intimacy. Using the popular iPhone Notes app, celebrities have begun to send their fans mea culpas after they make mistakes. Direct and imperfect, these messages can seem natural and fallibly human, which makes the public feel connected to the celebrity. However, if their fans get the impression that the apology isn't heartfelt, it backfires. A curated, overly careful apology doesn't communicate the same sense of personal sincerity and makes people feel manipulated.[20]

Another way to make your apology seem less genuine is to present a lot of defensive details. A Cambridge, Massachusetts, school committee member learned this lesson after she used the N-word at a school meeting—to illustrate a point about its use—which upset students. She attempted to say she was sorry, but the students rejected her apology as insincere. According to the students' teacher, the official tried to explain herself for ten minutes before she got to her apology. "In hindsight," she said, "I realized I should have simply conveyed my apologies."[21] Complicated, lengthy statements detract from the most important message about your responsibility and make your regret less believable.

When the United Nations finally issued a partial apology for the cholera disaster in Haiti, commentators tended to focus on outgoing secretary-general Ban Ki-moon's omissions. Not only did he stop short of taking responsibility for introducing cholera in the first place—which is documented to have arrived by way of Nepalese aid workers—but his statement also followed several years of pressure to hold the UN accountable. (According to the Step Two guidelines, described previously, we can see that these are serious drawbacks.) The *Guardian* called it a "half-apology" because Mr. Moon expressed regret only for the insufficient response to the outbreak in Haiti.[22] However, Adrian Walker, a *Boston Globe* columnist, wrote that Mr. Moon's statement "was cheered by the Haitians themselves as a sincere expression of contrition." He quoted human rights activist Brian Concannon as saying that "the victims spontaneously broke into applause. The Haitians picked up that he was really sorry. And the sincerity was enough to trump the fact that [the apology] was limited."[23]

The most crucial thing people who've been hurt need is for their pain to be seen and cared about. That isn't the whole story, of course, but if you can communicate empathic understanding and sincere regret, you're on your way to an effective apology.

Don't use "I'm sorry" for other purposes. Earlier, we touched on two forms of "I'm sorry" that are not amends. One, the condolence, arises out of kindness and sympathy and usually is appreciated. The other, the habitual, reflexive "I'm sorry," clogs up our conversations. These "I'm sorrys" may distract from needed apologies, and they may have deleterious effects on how you are viewed in professional settings. Communications consultant Donna Moriarty wrote that they can "undermine your authority and your confidence, portray you as weak and indecisive, and even damage your credibility."[24]

Habits are very hard to change, but if you customarily follow a request or suggestion with an "I'm sorry," you might want to make an effort to remove this verbal tic from your vocabulary. Consider practicing by adding a pause after you've spoken the first part of a more assertive message. For people trying to change a habit of speech, I recommend that when you feel tempted to say the habitual phrase, you imagine clapping your hand over your mouth. Sometimes actually doing that is effective. You might also enlist a friend to help you notice when you make a pseudo-apology. Personally, I've been trying to substitute "thank you" for "I'm sorry," because it often reflects my meaning more accurately. For example, if I have to interrupt a conversation for a bathroom break—which is not uncommon for me—I try to remember to say, "Thank you for waiting" or "I appreciate your patience" rather than "I'm sorry."

Better late than never (usually). The #MeToo movement awakened memories of past sexual harassment or assault for many people. For most, these were terribly unhappy, traumatic events, so the new reminders evoked reexperiencing and required fresh coping. Among my therapist colleagues' patients and in my own practice, many people felt forced to revisit painful memories. For others, these reexaminations of the past raised guilty feelings, even if they hadn't perpetrated mistreatment themselves, but had failed, for example, to support a peer in college who reported being sexually assaulted.[25]

In a column in WBUR's ideas blog *Cognoscenti*, I encouraged men to reconsider their own behavior from earlier in their lives, to reexamine what once might have seemed acceptable in the light of a new understanding of consent that is reaching the mainstream. I believe that "it behooves good men to make whatever repairs they can related to their own regrettable behavior" because it makes a difference to them and to those whom they hurt.[26]

It was in the context of the Senate confirmation hearings for now Supreme Court justice Brett Kavanaugh—which involved allegations of sexual assault—that the *New York Times* invited men to send in their memories of adolescent sexual misconduct. Among the hundreds of men who wrote in, several specifically mentioned apologies, either the one they wished they'd made, the one they would make if they had the chance now—even decades later—or one that they tried to make in the printed letter itself, directly to the person they regretted mistreating. I'm not aware of whether any of these accounts actually helped the victims, but they presented public models of people holding themselves accountable—finally.[27]

Dan Harmon, a successful television showrunner, took delayed responsibility for harmdoing by way of a widely seen YouTube video. Six years after he mistreated a woman writer who worked for him, he tried to make things right. Originally, because he'd been attracted to her, he'd made her life miserable. First, he favored her unfairly over the rest of the writing team, and, when she finally convinced him she wasn't romantically interested in him, he engaged in extensive verbal abuse and harassment. "What a jerk," you might think, and you'd be right. Ultimately, though, with the help of women colleagues and a book his therapist recommended—the excellent *On Apology* by psychiatrist Aaron Lazare—he faced what he'd done.

According to Megan Ganz, the writer he'd targeted, he issued what she called "a master class in how to apologize." It's worth watching the seven-and-a-half-minute video because it demonstrates important aspects of a good apology. He made no excuses, took complete responsibility for his actions—described in considerable detail—and urged other men not to make his mistakes in their treatment of women.

126

Step Two: Say It and Mean It

Here, though, I have to point out that Ms. Ganz crucially shaped his apology. Via Twitter, she gave him feedback that his initial statements were inadequate. He'd first written things like "Sorry for being a bad boss" and he'd asked her to help him find relief. Both Ms. Ganz and Mr. Harmon deserve credit for sticking with the process until he did it well.[28] In Chapter 9, we'll examine other ways the potential recipient can influence the apology she or he needs.

Another delayed apology had more ambiguous results. In 2016, when Peter DeMarco's wife suffered a catastrophic and ultimately fatal asthma attack, he and her family were heartbroken. During the early days of his grief, Mr. DeMarco, a *Boston Globe* reporter, wrote a lovely letter of appreciation to the hospital and especially the ICU staff who'd taken care of Laura Levis during a coma that preceded her death. His thank-you letter was widely circulated, even appearing in the *New York Times*. At that time, he had no idea what had actually happened to her the night of her attack.

As he mourned, Mr. DeMarco tried to make sense of the events that led to his wife's death. It ended up taking two years of research for him to piece together the story of the time before her hospital admission. He was astounded and enraged to learn that Ms. Levis had been unable to get into a locked emergency room door. She had tried to make it to another door but collapsed just feet from it. The outside area was not well lit; a nurse who was asked to check outside didn't see her when she briefly looked out from the doorway. No one searched outside. In addition, although she'd called 911 from outside the hospital and related her circumstances and location, first responders couldn't locate her quickly and accurately. Those crucial minutes when no one found her made the difference in her survival.

For two years, Cambridge Health Alliance, the hospital system that runs both the Somerville Hospital, with the tragically inaccessible emergency room, and the Mount Auburn Hospital, where Ms. Levis received ICU care, did not talk to Mr. DeMarco. They accepted his public appreciation yet didn't acknowledge their contributions to his wife's death. No one offered him or her family information about that night, much less an apology. Without their help, he searched all he could, including police and emergency responders' records. His account of what happened, including all the errors he could uncover, appeared in the *Boston Globe Magazine*.[29]

Ten days after the publication of the story of Ms. Levis's death—more than two years after it happened—hospital executives finally initiated a meeting with the widowed husband. They'd previously refused to comment on his wife's care, citing litigation concerns. At this point, his stirring story had reached a wide audience and the court of public opinion had found the hospital system at fault. In the two-hour meeting, he asked the hospital leaders his questions about what had happened and what had been preventable. Patrick Wardell, chief executive of Cambridge Health Alliance, acknowledged Mr. DeMarco's "horrible pain," said he was sorry, and took personal responsibility for the tragedy. Chief Medical Officer Assaad Sayah told him about the many changes they had instituted, based on their failure to take care of Ms. Levis in her time of need. Mr. DeMarco stated that he was grateful, after all that time, to hear directly from them. "They offered me accountability today, by admitting their mistakes, by finally doing the right thing."

Mr. DeMarco reportedly found the eventual apology helpful, but he also had grappled in the interim—without help from those responsible for the harm—with how to heal and how to honor his beloved. During those two years, the hospital's failure to help him understand what had happened to his wife had left her loved ones with an incomplete story.[30]

You can see that late apologies may still be genuinely helpful; they can indeed be enough for some people and under some circumstances. But a responsible statement of regret that came sooner—and independent of external pressures—could have spared people who had already been hurt badly from unnecessary additional pain and confusion.

HOW *NOT* TO SAY "I'M SORRY"

You've probably issued inadequate Step Twos yourself. You may have phrased your statement of regret in one of these misguided ways:

1. Any Step Two that begins with "I'm sorry, but..." is likely to fail. Whatever follows the "but" ("I didn't mean to hurt you," "it was a joke," "you're too sensitive," "you started it") invalidates the apology.
2. Similarly, "I'm sorry if..." ("anything I said upset you," "anyone was bothered by what I did," "you thought I meant *x* or *y*") suggests that the apologizer doesn't really take responsibility for any actual injury.
3. Use of the passive voice: "I'm sorry that..." ("you were hurt by how things unfolded," "that unfair things were allowed to happen," "that I was forced by a bad situation to do what I'd promised not to do") fails to show that you hold yourself accountable for your actions or their results.
4. An apology statement that ends with "not my fault" or "I didn't mean it" decidedly doesn't take personal responsibility.
5. A statement that skips the actual effect on the other person and focuses on their (misguided) reaction: "I'm sorry that..." ("you got so mad at me," "you see it that way," "you're so upset by this") might sound like an apology, but it isn't one.
6. Vagueness also is a big drawback if you want to take a good Step Two: "I'm sorry..." ("for what happened," or "for any hurt caused," or "for poor communication").
7. An attempt to stop the conversation, rather than understand the

injury ("I said I'm sorry; what more do you want?"), or to require that the other person move on ("Please forgive me; I can't stand you being mad at me anymore") won't be satisfying and won't resolve the problem.

8. "Sorry about that!" conveys an informal attitude of "Oops, too bad, dude! Do I look like I care?" It diminishes both the apologizer and the hurt person.

9. Lengthy, complex statements that are so obscure no one can tell what's being said, like the government's "Whereas" statement to Native Americans or statements that explain the circumstances or any other considerations at length, are not real apologies.

10. No rationalizations or justifications fit in Step Two. Save them for later if you still need them.

In their apology processes, Monique, Margo, and David all made it clear that they cared about their loved ones' hurt. They acknowledged how they'd contributed to it, expressing empathy and regret. By the time they took Step Two, none of them said anything in defense of their behavior, made excuses, or argued about their intentions or character.

PRACTICE SCRIPTS FOR STEP TWO

- "I'm so sorry that my drinking too much / arguing with your sister / arriving so late / making light of a serious occasion ruined such an important day for you. There is no excuse good enough."

- "It's my fault I didn't plan ahead better so the train delay wouldn't have made me so late. I'm really sorry."

- "I should have realized how much it would mean to you for me to come with you to your cousin's funeral. I'm so, so sorry you had to face that hard time on your own."

- "I can see how deeply my attempt at humor actually hurt you. I wish I could take it back."

- "I wish I'd thought to ask you before ordering the nonrefundable tickets. I can see that I've put you in an awful position."

CHAPTER 6

Step Three: Debts, IOUs, and Making Things Whole

The relevant question for Step Three is: What, if anything, would make up for the hurt or the wrong itself? What kind of restitution, reparations, or amends would restore balance or fairness that's been disrupted?

The legal concept of making a plaintiff "whole" usually refers to returning an injured party to her, his, or their original financial status. In personal relationships, the goal of restitution or reparations may be seen as making the *relationship* whole, restoring trust, or even strengthening the connection. As such, most personal reparations are not monetary (or not wholly so). Reparations may not seem to apply to intimate partnerships, but Step Three can inspire creative solutions that get to the heart of the damage.

In the relationship realm, sometimes just the expression of sincere penitence is enough to begin healing, but some form of restitution is usually necessary for a thorough process. Between individuals, Step Three could include "setting the record straight" in the eyes of other people, taking a second (or third) chance to get something right, or providing material goods that have symbolic or monetary value, or both.

When they arrived in my office, Sam had no idea why Mario was so upset. He had admitted that he was sorry he'd made them very late to a family gathering a couple of months previously. They had argued about how unreliable he could be about time commitments. But Mario had stayed just as upset after his partner had uttered the phrase "I'm sorry." As time passed, the characteristically unruffled Mario became increasingly irritable. Their usual good-natured sparring turned sharper and stilted.

I turned to Sam and coached him to take Step One and ask Mario what had happened for him that day—and since.

In response, Mario's tone was clipped and his posture tight. "You know I was looking forward to celebrating Aunt June's birthday. I'd been writing that toast for weeks. You remember, right?"

Sam nodded. "Of course."

"You actually helped me one night when I was working on it. Remember, you reminded me of that roller-coaster story about Deb to put in?" Mario turned to me. "But at the party, we weren't just a little late. We were so late, by the time we walked in, the 'happy birthdays' were already done and everyone had moved on to dessert. I was really disappointed and pissed at Sam."

"I get that," Sam spoke up, "but why can't you let it go? It's been months! And I said I was sorry that night."

"I know. But I'm still mad. And I'm still upset about it. In fact, I feel worse and worse about the whole thing. I keep thinking about how I let Aunt June down." He filled in background for me: "She's always been really good to me. She was the one who stood by me when my parents couldn't handle my coming out. I've never been able to do much to repay her, which is why I wanted to give her this seventieth birthday party. Her kids, my cousins, contributed, but it was my idea."

"I'd forgotten that." Sam looked pained.

"I actually promised her..." Mario took a moment to swallow and regain composure. "I told her I'd be hosting the evening. I told her my toast would make her laugh, so she wouldn't have to feel self-conscious."

Sam leaned toward his husband and gently rubbed his shoulder. Because Mario had largely avoided placing blame, Sam could also avoid most of his defensiveness and therefore feel natural empathy. He expressed regret in a more careful, thorough way (Step Two) than he had before: **"I'm really sorry I wrecked that important night for you. I wish I hadn't lost track of time and made you so late."**

Mario nodded and said, "Thanks," but his smile was a sad one. His anger had deflated, but it was clear that something was still bothering him.

After a minute, I stepped in. "That's a much better beginning to an apology, Sam. Does that help, Mario?"

He nodded again but didn't look any happier. Without the energy of his ire at Sam, he seemed left only with disappointment and his own regret.

We sat in silence for a bit.

"What do you think would help you feel better about this whole thing?" I asked.

"I don't think there is anything. The moment has passed."

At the risk of bringing out more hard feelings, I continued, "What is the worst part of this for you *now*, Mario?"

Mario considered his words. We waited.

"I guess there are two things. One is I didn't get to tell her how much I appreciate her—in this particular way that I had really looked forward to. It's not the end of the world, I know, and I will be able to tell her in other ways..."

I didn't let him undermine his message too much. "Okay, that's one thing. What's the other one?"

Step Three: Debts, IOUs, and Making Things Whole

"I'm embarrassed to say...that I'm embarrassed...I know, I know...that everyone saw us come in late, including her. I didn't want to hurt her feelings, but also it seemed disrespectful and rude and I don't want to be seen as that kind of person." He shrugged to Sam. "I know we've talked about this before. I wish I didn't care about how people see me, but I do."

Sam thought for a moment, then said, **"Look, I know it matters to you and I didn't take that into consideration with my woeful time management. It's definitely not your fault that this happened. It's totally on me."**

Another pause.

Sam had begun the hard work of taking responsibility for the pain that Mario was feeling. He had listened sincerely and had honestly expressed remorse for what he did that hurt his partner. He held himself accountable in words. But, as Brandi Miller, a campus minister and justice program director, wrote in *HuffPost*, "The acknowledgement of wrong by itself isn't a righting of wrong." She's addressing the problem of white people who seem to apologize after they've harmed people of color "but do nothing to rectify the damage they've caused,"[1] but, in my view, this truth holds everywhere else, too.

The familiar expression "Words are cheap" is relevant here. An apology has to be backed up with something of value and, if possible, by something that fits the harm done. Doug Conant, former CEO of Campbell Soup, once said, "You can't talk your way out of something you behaved your way into. You have to behave your way out of it."[2] The words "I'm sorry" are not magic words that make things right. Despite the difficulty many of us have uttering those words, they are simply not enough in themselves. Further, those two words can distract us from the rest of the real, necessary work.

This reminds me, again, of that crucial lesson regarding children: When we teach them that saying the words "I'm sorry" is all an apology takes, we miss an opportunity for them to learn about repair. We could instead raise the question of what can be done to make the situation right. How can we fix what got broken? How can you make up for what you did?

I waited for Sam to take up the task of fixing the problems he'd created for Mario.

After a minute, he ventured, **"Can I call Aunt June and tell her the reason you weren't there at the beginning? She should know it was my doing, not yours."**

Mario nodded but didn't speak, still feeling vulnerable from having stirred up distressed feelings.

"For that matter, I could send around a follow-up to the party—"

"Oh, I don't know about that," Mario interrupted. "We have to be really careful with some of the cousins."

"I know. I can be light and funny, **telling everyone, 'It was so great to see you! My only regret is that I screwed up by making us so late** we didn't get anywhere near enough time with you all.'" His voice had picked up a quasi-formal, British lilt during his message, after which he returned to his normal tone: "Of course, I wouldn't send anything without your okay. What do you think?"

Mario's smile had broken out during Sam's funny delivery of his suggestion. "That would be really nice of you."

Some form of Sam's terrific offer to "clear the record," so others knew what happened, is a frequent part of reparative efforts. In many contexts, a false narrative can cause damage, but you can help a person regain the credibility that you caused them to lose. If someone has been blamed unfairly (particularly for more serious offenses than Mario's lateness), making the true story known—by writing a letter, speaking directly to the parties involved, or even writing or speaking in a public forum—can correct an injustice. Your words can exonerate someone who doesn't deserve blame. (See the "Setting the Record Straight" section later in this chapter.)

Although they'd reached a better place, it was clear to all of us that the problem wasn't fully solved. Sam asked, "What else can we do?"

His question is a good one, because it invites Mario to help shape the repair, but it shouldn't be up to Mario to come up with solutions. I asked, "Any other thoughts, Sam?"

"I've got an idea. **How about a do-over? What if we take her out to a special dinner and you can finally deliver your toast?** Maybe we could book a private room, so you can stand up and present it. Or we could make her one of her favorite dinners at home?"

Mario agreed, "I think that would be great. I'd actually love to do that."

Sam's suggestion showed not only that he was willing to make amends, but also that he was considering Mario's specific experience. Because he paid attention to Mario's persistent wish to express appreciation to his aunt, Sam's proposed solution let him be an active part of repairing the damage.

SECOND CHANCES

Sometimes a makeup occasion, another chance to try again at something that went badly the first time, can seem silly and self-conscious, but often it is more powerful than you might anticipate.

If you've blown an important event or forgotten an anniversary or birthday, it can be a great idea to plan a corrective one. One mom wrote to the "Tell Me About It" syndicated column in the *Washington Post* to describe how she and her kids responded to letting down her husband one Father's Day. On a subsequent day, they put on a D.A.D., a Dad Appreciation Day, filled with activities he especially enjoyed and a homemade banner. "Because of the effort and surprise, it turned out to be his favorite 'father's day.'"[3]

A friend told me a similar story about the time she forgot her husband's birthday. She and her children filled the following week with gifts from each of them and his favorite desserts. Years later, she still affectionately relates the story of the time he let her make up for her mistake. In another family, the mother was usually disappointed by her birthday, which occurred just before Christmas when everyone was preoccupied with the holiday. (I can relate; mine is December 27.) Her family began to surprise her on her half birthday in late June—which she loved. Eventually, that became her regular birthday celebration. These stories all demonstrate the extraordinary power of Step Three—not only by making up for an error, but also by bringing people closer together and creating new opportunities for bonding.

For Lisa and Philip, whose wedding had taken place under a dark cloud because of Lisa's worry about what had happened at the bachelor party, the disappointing events from years ago couldn't themselves be undone. What had been lost were the potential and pleasure of a special day—and nearly their marriage. Once Philip had learned about how he'd affected his wife, Lisa, he felt bad that he'd let her down. He said, **"I can't tell you how sorry I am that I didn't talk to you on what should have been our perfect day. I could have made all this better by just telling you the truth then. Nothing happened. I hate how much time we've lost and how bad you've felt."** But that was only Step Two. Was there a way to make up for it?

During a later session, they shared a moment of particularly close understanding. Philip got on one knee on my office carpet. He addressed her with the nickname he hadn't called her in years.

Step Three: Debts, IOUs, and Making Things Whole

"LeeLee, will you marry me? Will you give me another chance to make our marriage be what we want it to be?"

She was crying too hard to speak but took his hand and nodded.

Together, they decided to recelebrate their wedding, hoping to improve their chances for a relatively clean slate. They planned the event, bought special clothes, and invited family and close friends. They even picked out new rings to commemorate their renewed commitment. As they worked on their plan, they found themselves warming further to each other.

THE FIX HAS TO FIT

The most successful kinds of redo efforts are the ones that fit the specific situation that caused the rift. Whatever you find to make up for some wrong or hurt should be proportional to the harm. It should satisfy the right problem.

Carolyn was unhappy that her husband hadn't listened to her about what mattered to her in the choice of a new car. Jim was a "car guy" and had strong opinions about what models and features were desirable. He negotiated a good deal and was very pleased with himself when he presented her with a car he thought was the best option. She appreciated his effort and didn't want to rain on his parade. But she didn't like the car. It was too big, too "fancy," and too silver. At first, she was prepared to make the best of it, but when she discovered that Jim had also preset the car's radio to the stations he liked, she was angry. The car was clearly "his."

Turning toward me, Carolyn complained that Jim didn't care what she thought, didn't value her opinions, never paid any attention to what she said. In his defense, Jim reminded her of all the ways their house was set up according to her preferences. I asked him to listen to her again. To her, I recommended that she tell him how she felt specifically about the car situation, omitting the absolute statements, such as that he never paid attention to what she said. After Step One, Jim understood how his choices regarding the car had unwittingly made her feel bad. He told her how sorry he was (Step Two).

The next week, Jim said, "I want you to drive whatever car you want. I have a suggestion about the whole situation. **Since I chose the Lincoln for you, maybe *I* should drive it. We can trade my car in. If you want me to, I'd be happy to go with you to look at cars you might like. I won't give my two cents unless you ask for it.**"

Carolyn was touched that he'd heard her dissatisfaction and was willing to shift his position. "Okay, that would be great. Thank you, honey."

After a beat, she added, "Would you still handle the negotiations, though?"

Sometimes the reparative action fits because it is an actual replacement or return of a lost object. If you've taken someone else's belonging, you should return it. If you've lost or damaged someone else's belonging, you should replace it. If the belonging can't be replaced, you must find a satisfactory substitute or an object whose value is symbolic. You are obligated to restore to the person the "wholeness" they held before you cost them something, or to correct a deficit you caused.

For example, bicyclist Mike Friedman reached out to the man he'd beaten unfairly in a race fifteen years earlier. He told Ian Dille that his cheating had eaten at him all this time. He looked into his eyes and said, **"You were right"** and **"I'm sorry"** (Step Two). Further, he made two kinds of restitution. He provided us with an example of replacing an actual, but also symbolic, object. Years after he cheated Mr. Dille of victory, Mr. Friedman presented the "Captain America" shirt he'd been awarded after the race to the man who should have won it. In addition, he demonstrated how to set the record straight—literally—by petitioning the governing body to correct the official record, so that it reflected Mr. Dille as the victor.[4]

One of my favorite restitutive behaviors came when Attiya Khan held her ex-boyfriend accountable on her terms. After he told her he was sorry for having beaten her regularly when they were teens, she asked him to participate in a film project. He agreed to appear in on-camera conversations about the physical abuse that had lasted throughout their two-year relationship, twenty years earlier. Across two years, they talked with each other, sometimes with a therapist present and sometimes in places where they'd been together in the past. Her documentary, *A Better Man*, premiered in 2017.[5] The content, including descriptions of the actual physical harm and the lack of help from neighbors, is gripping and painful. For Ms. Khan, telling the story of her mistreatment—with her ex-boyfriend's cooperation—allowed her to begin to heal. Her nightmares ended; her fears lessened.[6] It's not clear whether her ex-boyfriend, called Steve in the documentary, became "a better man," but he did provide the restitution she needed.[7]

In addition to making your restitution offer fit the harm done, you also have to bear in mind that the way you fix the problem should be a method that suits the person you hurt. Different people prefer different approaches for any kind of communication. Maybe your partner or friend or family member doesn't like expensive gifts or physical affection. Even if those things communicate in a way that would make you feel good, it behooves you to speak in the language the other person can hear. Often, it's not the same language you yourself might prefer. Is there a kind of action or material provision that will convey your feeling and repair things for this *particular* person?[8]

Remember Margo, who had taken a "break" from her friend and reawakened Annie's painful family experience? Margo found a creative fix that addressed the nature of the hurt she caused her friend. As the two of them found their way back toward greater ease in each other's company, Annie spoke more freely than she ever had about the loss of connection to her family. She showed Margo a treasured, cracked photograph and yellowed lacework from her grandmother, who had been a warm, loving presence in her early childhood. Margo raised the idea of Annie visiting her grandmother's hometown in Italy as an opportunity to connect more with her family roots. Familiar with Annie's limited financial resources, Margo began a gentle offer to pay for her friend's trip. Initially, Annie was reluctant, but a year later they made plans to travel together as Margo's gift for Annie's fiftieth birthday. The gift made emotional sense between them because it helped heal the same kind of hurt—a disconnection from close people—that Margo had caused.

SETTING THE RECORD STRAIGHT

Setting the record straight may come in the form of publicly accepting blame or owning up to your responsibility or behavior. Sam's plan to make sure Aunt June and the family didn't blame Mario for their lateness is a small-scale example of this type of restitution. So is the bicycle racer's correcting the record to reflect the rightful winner.

Making public a private harm or shame can also lead to support and additional restitution for an injured person. Memorializing someone whose story was lost is another way to help make reparations. Regardless of whether you were the person who caused the harm or hid the history, you can take this kind of reparative action. In this way, you may be able to prevent an injustice from continuing and help others move beyond an injury. In the world of social media, mistaken or false information can go viral quickly, which can make setting the record straight particularly urgent.

Public statements by leaders, on behalf of governments, can provide this kind of restitution, beginning with the acknowledgment of past harms. When Canadian prime minister Justin Trudeau issued an apology to LGBTQ2 citizens for decades of mistreatment, he also made sure to clear the literal, official record: Laws that had prevented expunging specific criminal records were changed, allowing for past discriminatory convictions arising from sexual orientation to be erased. What this and other initiatives that accompanied his public statement did was to begin to make amends. Healing can begin if someone states their regrets, but it can't continue without actual restitution. This holds for many personal apologies, too. Like Prime Minister Trudeau, you may speak sincerely, but if you don't also enact real change—in this case, take action to alter the criminal records that were part of the harm done—your words, however moving, mean little.

Recently, French president Emmanuel Macron also moved toward reparations by breaking with his country's previous policy in which leaders avoided acknowledgment of government-caused harm. He formally recognized the French military's systemic use of torture during the Algerian War of the 1950s and '60s. Further, he took specific restitutive action regarding the historical record. He called for opening the archives that tell the stories of many people who went missing during this conflict. His decree read that the general dispensation is **"so that everyone—historians, families, associations—can consult the archives for all those who disappeared in Algeria."** Being allowed to know the truth about what happened to your loved ones is powerful in this circumstance, as it was in the Truth and Reconciliation Commission hearings. In many cases, the information in the records was upsetting and disturbing, and certainly painted the French government in a negative light. But Mr. Macron's actions sent the signal that healing pain was more important than saving face.

French historian Benjamin Stora said that Mr. Macron's decision represented a move away from "the silence of the father," France's historic avoidance of its colonial past.[9] The president's Step Two statement of acknowledgment directly addressed previous harms that have held his country back from healing. But, further, his Step Three demonstrated how to heal the added damage of *having hidden the truth of past harms*. His initial statement could have been meaningful on its own, but it would have been far less helpful without this step toward restitution.

These leaders found meaningful ways to repair harmful actions of their governments and fellow citizens and, by doing so, provided us with a model. We, too, may be able to tackle our overdue personal apologies. We, too, can follow our statements of regret with real restitution, including—if it's indicated—"correcting the record." We, too, may be able to reveal or clarify the truth.

COLLABORATION

Makeup surprises can be nice because they show that the other person is thinking about you and wants you to be happy.

For example, flowers, a typical apology gift, may serve as a nice peace offering that opens the door to a more thorough apology. However, they may also make the recipient feel that she or he has to make the sender feel appreciated. Again, the relevant question to think about is, What would actually make up for the mistake or hurt? When possible, restitutive efforts ought to be collaborative.

After a medical error that causes harm, some doctors and institutions reach out to patients and their families and ask what they need. The CARe (Communication, Apology, and Resolution) protocol requires the staff to first address any immediate needs of the patient and family. They don't wait until there is a malpractice claim made to begin learning what people need. But the longer-term financial needs of the patient are also addressed as collaboratively and quickly as possible. We saw this kind of conversation lead to a quicker and more satisfying outcome for the patient from Chapter 1, Ms. Wagner, the woman who survived breast cancer and who finally felt heard. She received funds for her sons' educations in a timely manner.

Whenever possible, you must involve the injured party—or their representatives—in any plan to make the most effective recompense. A particularly powerful example of this challenge is found in the recent efforts by institutions to examine and make reparations for their participation in and benefits from inhumane customs, particularly slavery. For example, in 2015, the president of Georgetown University, John DeGioia, appointed a university committee to address the school's roots in slavery. In addition to its historical dependence on slave labor since its founding, Georgetown had sold 272 enslaved people in 1838 and sent them to Louisiana. In 2016, Dr. DeGioia endorsed several recommendations from the study group: a formal apology, the founding of an institute for the study of slavery, the erection of a public memorial to the enslaved people whose labor benefited the institution, and the renaming of two buildings after African Americans. One of the people after whom a building was renamed, Isaac Hawkins, was in the group of enslaved workers shipped away in that transaction almost two hundred years earlier. As part of the university's amends, Dr. DeGioia announced an additional initiative for preferential admissions to the descendants of all the enslaved people who labored at Georgetown.

Although these were powerful first restitutive actions, since the announcement, there have been important critiques. One came from a group of the descendants who pointed out that they were not involved in the committee's deliberations, and many were not invited to the formal announcement. Some suggested that scholarships should also be offered to descendants. The president proposed a new committee for the creation of the public memorial, one that will include descendants, as well as access to genealogical information in the university's archives.[10]

Although some descendants appreciate the new elements and

are pleased to have additional information about their family histories, others view these changes as insufficient restitution. In January 2018, university and Jesuit leaders reached out to descendants and proposed **"a framework for long-term dialogue, partnership and collaboration."**[11] Dialogue may lead to more effective solutions, but it serves the purpose of repair only if it leads to action, rather than further delay in making things right.

Some voices among the descendant community and academia raise the idea that financial reparations are specifically indicated. Sociologist Tressie McMillan Cottom has praised Dr. DeGioia's powerful acknowledgment (our Step Two) but points out that effective restitution must be specific to the harm that's being addressed, in this case, uncompensated labor by enslaved people. Preferred admissions may lead to opportunity for some strong students, but she likened it to admitting you owe someone money and then repaying them with lottery tickets.[12]

In April 2019, two-thirds of Georgetown students voted to pay financial reparations to the descendants of the 272 enslaved people sold in 1838. The nonbinding referendum called for funds to be generated by a fee that applies to all current undergraduates.[13] This conversation continues.

A challenging aspect of the Georgetown situation is that the institution is trying to right wrongs that happened to people who are no longer with us. In the case of slavery, there is a clear argument to be made that descendants have also been harmed directly by the financial and societal legacies of the evil institution. Vicarious reparative attempts can and should still be as collaborative as possible. Descendants and others affected by the consequences of historical harms should have a chance to participate in decisions about restitution.

Recently, Tamara Lanier, a descendant of a formerly enslaved man called Renty, sued Harvard University for the return of daguerreotype images of her relative. Louis Agassiz, a nineteenth-century professor, had arranged for and displayed photographs of mostly naked enslaved people as part of his effort to establish the inferiority of people of African descent. In response to Ms. Lanier's claim, a group of Mr. Agassiz's descendants in turn petitioned the university in support of her position. Representing the group, Marian Moore, accompanied by Ms. Lanier, delivered a letter to the president of the university. There appear to be complicated legal issues and concerns about providing museum-level protection of fragile artifacts, but the overarching reality here was that two great-great-great-granddaughters walked side by side in an effort to heal harm caused to one man by another generations earlier.[14]

If you don't know how to make restitution, the best way to find out is to ask. To powerful men affected by the #MeToo movement, feminist lawyer Jill Filipovic suggests that they first focus on how to make amends, rather than how to return to power. If they are uncertain how to make their wrongs right, they can ask women who spend their lives thinking about these issues. She further recommends that they compensate the people who provide their expert help.[15]

Remember Dan Harmon, who made the effective YouTube apology? Initially, he had no idea how to face the harm he'd inflicted on Megan Ganz. Only after paying attention to the guidance from her was he able to drop his defensiveness and make a good apology. In the meantime, he also consulted with other female colleagues, asking them questions and listening to their answers, and he read a book about apologies. These are good collaboration aids, especially helpful if you are not in an ongoing relationship with the person you hurt.

As with Georgetown's efforts, even if you are trying to do the right thing in personal repair situations, you must check with the other person in the relationship that you want to heal. It's not a form of punishment; it's a way to build a new foundation of trust and communication as you work together to repair your relationship. Let the idea and act of reparation inspire a creative collaboration.

MAKING REPARATIONS HELPS YOU, TOO

Obviously, restitution is geared toward helping the one who's been harmed. Your task, as the apologizer, is to restore your partner, friend, or coworker to their status prior to their being harmed. Often, you have a chance to make things better than they were before. It may cost you something, but if you find a satisfying solution, everyone wins. When Margo took her friend to Italy, she was deeply happy that she'd found something meaningful she could give Annie to heal her friend's sad isolation from her family. She loved sharing the family reconnection with her. Likewise, Sam felt like a better partner when he arranged the dinner where Mario was finally able to give his aunt the appreciative speech he'd written for her.

In the religious rituals we read about in Chapter 3, the penitent person feels forgiven, or right with God, once they've provided restitution to someone they've harmed. We probably all understand the human sense of justice that requires you to restore or repair what you've damaged. That's one basic way that making restitution also restores the one who's caused harm. As you rebalance a wrong, you get to feel better about yourself.

In the 1990s, psychiatrist Jonathan Shay reintroduced the concept of "moral injury" into psychiatric literature. The term overlaps with PTSD but refers to a more specific result of doing something that violates a person's deep beliefs about what's morally right. In the case of soldiers with whom Shay worked, the problem often results from a conflict between competing values, for example, the sanctity of life versus loyalty to one's commanding officer. Following orders that lead to people's deaths is a prime cause of moral injury.[16] The veteran thus affected suffers from persistent guilt and shame, the lack of ethical clarity, and even the loss of a sense of what makes life meaningful. It's a terrible affliction that has been refractory to conventional therapies.

In a 2017 *New York Times* essay about veterans with this problem, Aaron Pratt Shepherd invokes philosopher Josiah Royce's writing about what's necessary to "treat" the aftermath of tragically irrevocable acts. Contrary to what you might think, the solution for this kind of ailment is not found through forgiveness or support from someone else. Dr. Shepherd recommends what he calls atonement, trying to fix something you've broken or to reunify something that's been torn apart. First the veteran has to identify which personal value or moral code was sacrificed in the proverbial or actual heat of battle. Then he or she begins a search for creative deeds that can help reclaim or restore the violated value.[17] For example, some veterans plagued by their actions that damaged civilian neighborhoods have devoted themselves to work with Team Rubicon, a veterans' organization that helps communities in distress overcome disasters and disadvantages.[18] Efforts to make amends could also include political endeavors to reduce the presence of soldiers in civilian war zones or a renewed focus on good parenting or safe neighborhoods. The work itself appears to be therapeutic not only because it restores wholeness for the recipients of the help, but also because it restores the wholeness of the veteran.

HISTORICAL INEQUITIES: NOT YOUR FAULT, BUT STILL YOUR RESPONSIBILITY

On larger scales, where your individual actions rarely seem connected to major negative outcomes, a crucial distinction exists between accepting blame for harmful actions and taking responsibility for addressing harm or its downstream effects. As David Brooks, conservative columnist, wrote recently, "Sometimes the costs of repairing sin have to be borne generations after the sin was first committed."[19]

"The costs of repairing" is exactly what restitution or reparation means. These costs can refer to compensation for victims of harm or loss, restoration to previous financial status, or making amends for injustice. In the United States, the issue of reparations for our two "original sins," the near annihilation of Native Americans and the enslavement of Africans, remains controversial. Many share a view I've seen written on Facebook: "I refuse to apologize for something that happened 150 years ago." I can see their point, if I accept the premise that an apology is the equivalent of accepting personal blame. Of course, *I* didn't personally seize Native Americans' land or kidnap people from Western Africa. *I* didn't redline neighborhoods or participate in cruel Jim Crow practices. *I* didn't force-march migrations of people far from home, send them to schools that robbed them of culture and language, or cheer on those who did. I abhor the effects of mass incarceration. You might ask, why should *I* apologize?

Here's the thing: My white father went to college and got his first home as a result of his service in World War II. Many loyal members of the armed forces were denied those opportunities because of their skin color. The wealth of white Americans (on average) has compounded over time, in addition to myriad other benefits I accrued, simply because I look a certain way. I was poor, but my opportunities and those of my children may have been completely different had I been a poor black or brown person. I personally have benefited from these historical realities.

From where I sit, personal benefit from injustice is as compelling a reason to take responsibility as is personal blame. While I did not create the powerful system that ranked—and ranks—some people as more valuable than others, one way to contribute to rectifying the past is taking my share of responsibility for changing the present and, we can hope, the future. Overall, it seems to me that the biggest overdue apology of our time is the one owed by white Americans to Americans of color. In her movie *Traces of the Trade*, filmmaker Katrina Browne reports on her white, northern family's involvement in the slave trade. At one point, she states that learning about the injustice makes a person naturally want to make things right, but it isn't guilt that drives that urge; it's grief.[20]

When people discuss changing the legacy of inequities, the question of how reparations can be made at this large a scale naturally arises. In his high-profile 2014 essay in the *Atlantic*, "The Case for Reparations," writer Ta-Nehisi Coates argues that centuries of slavery, followed by almost another two centuries of discriminatory laws and housing policies, call for direct US actions aimed at making things right. He makes a clear case that financial restitution for the descendants of enslaved African Americans is possible.[21]

In 2019, almost five years after he questioned the validity of Mr. Coates's assertions, *New York Times* columnist David Brooks published a changed perspective on the subject. After "traveling around the country . . . studying America's divides," he concluded that "reparations are a drastic policy and hard to execute, but the very act of talking about and designing them heals a wound and opens a new story."[22] The idea also returned to Congress in 2019, in the form of a bill that proposes a commission to study US reparations for slavery. This plan is similar to legislation introduced in 1989, thirty years earlier. The idea has come back around and appears to be gathering support again.

One of the challenges to considering reparations is how to structure and manage something that would affect so many Americans. Several academics have addressed the question. In 2019, Patricia Cohen, national economics correspondent for the *New York Times*, presented a survey of reparations concepts, including whom should be paid, how much they should receive, and what the economic impact of such restitution would be. She began with General William T. Sherman's promise to black Americans released from bondage, that they would be given "40 acres and a mule."[23] President Abraham Lincoln and Congress approved the arrangement, and forty thousand freedmen began to plant and build. Soon after President Lincoln's death, President Andrew Johnson rescinded the offer and took the land away. Once more, Congress tried to provide compensation, but it was vetoed by Mr. Johnson. Some reparations scholars have tried to assess the present-day value of those forty acres as a basis for financial restitution. If you find this model—or any other—reasonable, you may contribute your voice to the larger conversation about how the United States can best make reparations.

Aside from national policy, what can individuals do to make reparations for something as big as slavery? Recently, Michael Eric Dyson, professor and Baptist minister, wrote a book called *Tears We Cannot Stop*, in the form of a church service. He presents a long list of possible ways individual white Americans can contribute to righting the wrongs of our racial past. Among other methods, he recommends starting an individual reparations account, contributed to on a regular basis, that is used, for example, to provide support for a college student's textbooks or fairer compensation for workers you hire.[24] As I understand it, the idea is that you don't have to wait for large, institutional change before you participate in reparations efforts. As a white person trying to level the historically unfair field caused by disparate privilege, you could contribute to the increased well-being of others.

An apology restores balance to a relationship that's been damaged. A Step Three that is empathic or collaborative, or both, helps relationships build more trust and find more warmth.

Reparative actions appeal to our natural sense of justice and fairness. And a good apology also helps the apologizer restore balance within herself or himself. In response to "good guilt," a normal person—that is, a moral person—who takes responsibility for hurt and takes suitable restorative action feels less burdened. As with the soldiers suffering from moral injury, apologizers feel better about themselves and clearer about what matters most to them.

You may feel awkward approaching this step of an apology. Step Two, making your statement of regret, is hard enough, but at least it's familiar territory. You may never before have thought about this kind of restitutive action as an essential part of making amends. The good news is twofold: First, once you look for them, many fitting restitutions are evident. They often involve replacing something, redoing something, or repaying something owed. Second, you don't have to figure out your personal reparations alone. Ideally, your Step Three arises from conversation between you and the person(s) with whom you're trying to make things right.

PRACTICE SCRIPTS FOR STEP THREE

- "I want to help heal your hurt. I've got some ideas how. Can we talk about them?"

- "Is there something I can do to make up for how much my mistake hurt you?"

- "What would help you be able to trust me again?"

- "Will you please tell me if you see anything else I can do to make this right?"

- "I'd like to make sure that everyone who was affected by what happened understands that I'm responsible for it. Can we talk about how I can do that?"

CHAPTER 7

Step Four: Never Again!

Just because you've apologized and made up for a specific hurt you inflicted, how can anyone be sure it won't happen again? The "injured party" often remains wary of repetition. Can people really move on if the same thing can happen again? Is it really repaired if the conditions that produced the hurt still exist? Step Four is the one most often missed by apologizers, even those skilled in relationship repair. But it is where the crucial result resides.

Beyond the cognitive biases we've talked about throughout this book is the overwhelming tendency to continue thinking and doing what we already have thought and done. Not only individual habits but also patterns between people acquire inertial force. As the common understanding goes, if you want to predict future behavior, look at past behavior.

What I have also seen, however, is that people—as well as relationships—can change.

In his later years, Simon had a spiritual awakening that led him to reevaluate many aspects of his life. The biggest one concerned his relationship with his youngest daughter, Suzanne, now a young adult. During his self-examination, he realized that he had expected too much companionship with her during her early adulthood. He feared that his need for her to occupy the role of a (nonsexual) partner, including frequent shared trips and evenings out, might have kept her too occupied with him and thereby interfered with her developing a normal social life. Since her junior year in high school, she'd been his go-to companion for sailing trips or concerts; he enjoyed her company greatly. But he'd been thinking of his own immediate interests rather than what would be best for her development. Now he worried it was his fault she'd evidenced little interest in romantic relationships.

Carefully, he sat her down and made his "discovery" known to her. In this case, he'd known more about the injury he caused than she had—consciously, at least. He told her how much he regretted his selfishness and blindness to what he was doing.

Suzanne told me that his confession made her incredibly uncomfortable. She'd known their relationship was unusual and her friends sometimes teased her about her "dates" with her father, but she'd never thought about their relationship in the way he described it. It took her awhile to get used to the new situation. It took her longer to understand. Nonetheless, it was astonishing how quickly his apology seemed to change her experience in the world. As soon as the next week, she began to notice that men her age were paying attention to her. She mused about the question of whether they had been looking at her with interest all along and she'd never noticed it, or she was sending out a different signal of some sort, which was eliciting attention.

Her father's statement of remorse had a manifest effect on Suzanne. Moreover, though, she saw that what made the biggest difference over time was that he followed through on his intentions; his changes held up even when she tried to return to their old pattern. First of all, he made concerted efforts to connect more regularly with his wife. Rather than fill his schedule with activities he shared with

Suzanne, he made a point to plan outings his real partner would enjoy. He scheduled regular check-in visits with his therapist, "to keep himself honest." Although they still saw each other and continued to have spirited, warm conversations and emails, he never again took his daughter to twosome evening events. Even when he was tempted to invite her to accompany him on trips and when she was "between boyfriends," he instead offered to pay for her travel with friends. He actively worked to prevent the pattern from redeveloping. He told her that walking her down the aisle at her wedding, several years later, was one of the happiest days of his life.

CHANGING THE SYSTEM

Step Four is about creating a set of parameters that will protect against an injury's recurrence, but in many instances it's also about changing the situation so that other, additional people don't get hurt in the future. An illuminating story about accountability that led to the prevention of future harm began with a terrible incident. In 1998, Brenda Tracy was raped and abused by four college football players in an hours-long nightmare. After she reported the crimes, the coach of the Oregon State University football team, Mike Riley, suspended his players for one game, saying they were "really good guys who made a bad choice."

Ms. Tracy experienced a hostile backlash from the community, which led her not to pursue criminal charges. Eventually, she became an advocate for rape survivors. Sixteen years after the assaults happened, she finally told her story to a reporter. In the intervening time, she was haunted by the coach's trivializing of what had been done to her. She said that she hated him more than she hated her rapists.

After she went public, Mr. Riley expressed his regret that he hadn't taken more action. He'd since moved to the University of Nebraska, and, at his invitation, Ms. Tracy came to meet him. They talked for two hours, during which time she said everything she needed to say and she asked him everything she needed to ask. According to her, he answered all her questions and apologized for not digging more into what happened and for not considering the impact on her life. Most important to her, she believed that he understood how much his decision had hurt her and that he would never do something like that again.

That encounter represented one man's change, one person's learning not to repeat harm. But Mr. Riley also invited Ms. Tracy to speak to his team, a "real-life talk...actually having someone talk about how things can change for everyone in a moment like that." She did, telling the players how much she had hated their coach and also pointing out that he didn't have to bring her there. She said, "This is what accountability looks like." She hoped the players could be "a good example in a very dark time for college football."[1] Together, she and Coach Riley contributed to improving the culture of entitlement that these college athletes live in, and they may have prevented future assaults. Since the Nebraska team talk, Ms. Tracy has spoken to many college teams, invited by their coaches.

She tells the young men, **"I'm not here because I think you are the problem—I'm here because I know you're the solution."**[2] It is her brave testimony that's making the difference here, of course, not Mr. Riley's behavior, but his amends kick-started this process.

Step Four is about solutions. Often, not only is it a search for ways to prevent the exact harm from happening again, but, as Ms. Tracy demonstrates, it's about finding solutions to the larger problem that led to the harm in the first place. This is precisely why your responsibility for preventing future harm can be relevant, whether or not you caused the previous harm. Like the young men Ms. Tracy meets with, you have the potential to find better ways to live as people who share a community.

* * *

Step Four: Never Again!

An impressive organization with the lengthy name the Massachusetts Alliance for Communication and Resolution following Medical Injury (MACRMI) offers training and extensive support for medical institutions trying to become more accountable. The prevention of future harm arises early and remains crucial in the hospitals' responses to patients and families. Detailed assessments of what went wrong are necessary in order to change procedures or policies that will ensure it won't happen again. Indeed, such assessments turn out to be very important to injured patients who want their suffering to contribute to some positive outcome.

At a recent MACRMI training about how to talk with an injured patient's family, Mr. Boothman, of the Michigan program we've heard about, said, "We know the most important person to them is their mother, but **right now the most important person to us is the next patient, the one we haven't hurt yet.**"[3] Although this approach may have become familiar to you in this book, it is actually a revolutionary change in perspective in medicine.

As recently as 2008, Beth Israel Deaconess Medical Center, a Harvard Medical School teaching hospital—which happens to be where I completed my clinical fellowship many years earlier—began to study what kinds of medical errors actually happen. Under CEO Paul Levy, they made mistakes completely transparent, including publishing them in candid terms on the hospital website.[4] This radical facing of medical errors was the hospital's strategy to make mistakes an open subject from which everyone can learn. After a medical error, a personal apology had to take place between the patient and the medical staff involved, but this larger open assessment occurred primarily on behalf of future patients.

Most of us do not direct institutions or find our unfortunate harm in the public domain like Brenda Tracy did, but we are part of various smaller groups and families. The old saying goes that we can't change anyone but ourselves, but it is also true that shifting our behavior—even to a small degree—can alter the pattern for others enough to protect a hurt person or prevent further damage. Almost always, when things are made more fair for one member of the group, everyone benefits.

Monique cared that her family had contributed to her husband Desmond's hurt feelings, so she talked with the children directly about respect and kindness. In addition to the ways she followed up on her personal commitments to him, she began to pay closer attention to what she was communicating to the rest of the family. She wasn't surprised to discover that they hadn't thought about the effects of their behavior.

During a discussion about inclusion, her nine-year-old daughter mentioned the Lowly Worm, a character in Richard Scarry's books for very young children. Despite his being labeled "lowly" and his actually being a worm, the character is cheerful. His size may put him at a disadvantage, but his jaunty attitude, embodied in his bow tie and one sneaker, makes him fun and sympathetic rather than pitied. The other kids "awwed" because they all associated him with early childhood pleasure. They remembered aloud some of his simple, silly adventures. For a few weeks, "lowly worm" became their affectionate term for someone who's feeling small.

A year later, when Desmond was going through a challenging period at work, he began to feel depressed. One evening, he told the family he felt like the "lowly worm." The next morning, he was touched to find a friendly note to "LW" with a drawing of the worm wearing Desmond's customary sweatshirt. The kids' natural fondness for the character seemed to make them more receptive than they might have been otherwise. After that, "LW" became the shared moniker the whole family used to signal that they felt in need of support.

During their therapy work with me, Monique and Desmond together had also established a hand gesture for him to signal her when he was feeling left out and wanted to speak with her separately from the kids. The tug on his ear harkened to a lighter moment, which they hoped could defuse future tensions that might arise. As it turned out, he didn't need to use it. Due to Monique's good apologies, their relationship was in better shape. As Desmond developed more comfort and connection with the children, he found his own voice in the family. Both "LW" and his potential tug on the ear are examples of creating new patterns to circumvent or change habitual ways that hadn't worked so well for one or all members of the group.

REPEATED HARM

If you've hurt someone in the past and regretted it, you probably promised not to do it again. But if the hurt has happened again, Step Four is particularly crucial. Perhaps an additional error should not doom the whole enterprise, but neither should it go without serious focus. It's upsetting to find yourselves in the same mess you've landed in before. It takes deliberate work for anyone to change their stubborn habits. I've struggled to change my own.

Sometimes the "offender" asserts (and believes) that repeated hurtful actions are random, that is, not caused by any particular intention or feeling. However, if troublesome actions become a pattern, a larger conversation needs to take place. You owe it to the one who's hurt to find a better way to address the problem. Regardless of how you think about it, the tenth time you neglect to follow through on the same commitment lands differently than the first. So does your tenth "I'm sorry" that's not accompanied by change.

If the harm is associated with compulsive behavior (such as gambling, substance abuse, pornography), the apologizer usually needs mental health treatment. For some people, though, commitment to a twelve-step program can support change in addictive behavior as well as or more effectively than psychotherapy.

It should be pointed out here that being "in therapy"—attending sessions with a therapist—does not necessarily constitute making actual change that will last and should therefore, in itself, not satisfy Step Four. Even when people are motivated to change their behavior in a therapy setting, good intentions are often insufficient. For long-standing or imbedded habits, most of us require some kind of structured support or change of systems in order to maintain a new pattern of behavior.

When Mariah married her husband, James, he and his children lived in a town far from her job, so she added a regular couple of hours a day commuting. Always a planner, she worried about his young sons, for whom no college funds had been set aside. James and the boys operated on a much more laid-back approach to the future, so she felt that it fell to her to work more and save money. You could argue that it wasn't her responsibility, but it reflected the values she had grown up with, and it seemed to her like the best way to answer the need in her current family. Over my years of couples therapy, I've observed many people who "overfunction" in their partnerships in this way.

In the meantime, though, she became chronically tired from her heavy schedule. Periodically she told James how overworked and overwhelmed she felt. His response was always to feel terrible about the situation and to say he was so sorry and that she deserved better. But nothing changed. Eventually she developed a series of viral illnesses that she couldn't shake. As the first child started college, she continued to commute and work long hours. She felt that she couldn't stop herself until they finished school. It seemed to her that she was the only one looking out for everyone else. What made her feel even worse was that James didn't seem to be equally looking out for her best interests. After overfunctioning for years, she finally fell apart in a more major way: She became quite depressed, and, once she began crying, she couldn't stop. His response was to feel terribly guilty. He was ashamed that he had allowed her to hurt herself by overworking and taking on too much: "I'm afraid I can never be the husband you need."

In their marriage, Mariah and James had sort of divided up the emotional landscape, so that she held a certain kind of moral authority and he enacted the role of someone weaker, less able to provide for anyone but himself. In fact, though, James was a highly capable person and a caring father. But, as in many "blended" families, the two of them hadn't had the opportunity to establish a balanced two-person relationship. (Might we dispense with that term, "blended," and perhaps call them patchwork families or jigsaw-puzzle families? Blending is rarely what happens—but that's a topic for another book.)

James's repeated apology had stalled out because it consisted only of Step Two, expressing regret and shame. They hadn't been able to communicate more fully because his upset feelings usually flared and she characteristically gave up. So, despite the fact that he cared, they hadn't discussed any real changes that would have actually improved things. First, they both needed to learn how to listen to each other without getting driven off topic by their emotions. In particular, James sought support from a spiritual counselor to help him slow down his reactivity and maintain his cool. Using some new tools, he conducted a thorough Step One—listening without shifting the focus to himself. With room to show her vulnerability, Mariah told him how she felt without the recriminations that had begun to feel habitual. She felt "lonely" and "afraid that I'll end up alone, exhausted, and without money." In response to her vulnerability, he felt moved to make a more responsible apology. He could see more clearly his wife's need for a closer partnership and could understand better his role in her pain.

In an oversimplified view of their shift, James began to step up from a role of being weaker and Mariah began to step down from playing the strong, solo role. They both learned that he loved it when she asked for his help. It was hard for her to do, but she found herself enjoying his assistance with large and small things.

She told him how much she appreciated it. Positive cycles began to gain some momentum.

Their relationship really changed only when he could take more responsibility for actual improvement of her situation and protection of her well-being going forward. He had to practice helping her more; of equal importance, she had to practice letting him. Perhaps these changes sound simple, but they both took repeated efforts and time. James pledged not to let her contribute so much financially to the family. He took on an additional professional role and, in turn, helped her think through options for cutting her work hours. When the time came for the next child to attend college, he wouldn't accept the contribution she offered—thereby demonstrating his commitment to a different system for them.

They collaborated. James took real steps that helped improve Mariah's immediate life but also thought actively about how to protect against the old patterns' returning. They were both happier because they had created a new channel of communication that strengthened their relationship.

CRIMINAL JUSTICE

In the midst of an effort to repair harm in a relationship, you are probably motivated to preserve the good feelings and connection that result. You may work toward a satisfying mutual resolution with high hopes. Nonetheless, making change that lasts can be brutally challenging. Everyone's inclined to backslide, to regress to previous ways, so you need supports and help to keep up changes until they become your new habits.

Systems for supporting lasting change are built into some legal consequences of wrongdoing. Although they have morphed into complex, sometimes misguided arrangements, parole and probation were designed to help people who'd committed crimes to remain law-abiding.

The restorative justice movement directly aims to hold the offender accountable in a way that will help the person make changes that last. The Massachusetts program in which I volunteer, called Communities for Restorative Justice (yet another acronym: C4RJ), requires the "responsible party" to participate in weekly exercises that address head-on the impact of the offense. They also help the person examine thinking errors and develop a "character contract" about what kind of adult he or she wants to be.

In one local C4RJ case, a sixteen-year-old named Danny had impulsively gone into a neighbor's garage one Saturday, stolen a motorcycle, and ridden it around. Curtis, the homeowner, knew him and was understandably hurt and angry about it, as was his family. In addition, though, other neighbors were also disturbed by the theft from their safe-seeming street. The restorative justice process is designed to focus on the victim's needs, but also to be compassionate to *all* parties. Together, everyone involved constructed a contract that required Danny to pay for the motorcycle to be tuned up and polished; to engage in community service at a local youth center; and to write a thorough apology letter to everyone affected, including detailed descriptions of what he did and the effects of his actions on other people.

For Danny, as for many, this was the first time he'd had to reckon with this level of responsibility for his actions. The process requires serious work and was eye-opening for him. As with the apologies we've been talking about, when the restorative justice process is successfully completed, everyone benefits. What results is a more peaceful situation, potentially a better citizen, and a more connected community. In Danny's case, after the months-long process and apology letter, Curtis felt that he'd been made "whole."

As Danny completed his obligations, his perspective widened. Curtis's view of the offending boy changed, too; he appreciated

Danny's efforts so much that he hired him to work in his nearby gro-
cery store. There, Danny continues to have regular contact with his
neighbors, who have come to see him in a different light as well.

A first-time offender completes the restorative justice program
with no criminal record. Relatively few of the participants offend
again. In C4RJ's first nine years, participants had a rate of reoffending
(16 percent) between 43 and 59 percent of the recidivism rate across
the state (depending on which statewide estimate you use). This is an
example of Step Four, developing a set of actions that will stop a person from reoffending.[5]

Preventing repetition is especially important in the case of serious
harm, as in sexual violence. Indeed, by a margin of three to one, crime victims surveyed in 2016 want people held accountable not just through punishment, but through rehabilitation, mental health treatment, and community service.[6] As we heard in Chapter 3 from author Michelle Alexander, most victims of violent crimes would prefer restorative practices for
the persons who hurt them, rather than prison. They want change, not
punishment.

IS REDEMPTION POSSIBLE?

At base, the question of redemption comes down to whether
someone can change. Do we believe it's possible? Can we change the
way we see someone after viewing them in a certain light? What does
it take for us to think someone deserves a second chance; that is, when
do we allow them to redeem themselves?

Mistakes committed by people in the public eye tend to show
up in the media painted in extremes of good and bad, from harsh
condemnation to saintly exoneration. Of course, some behavior is just
unacceptable, but most human relationships and most human stories
are more complicated than what we can get in a brief news account

or gossip. However, we're tempted to think we know the whole story or the basic truth and therefore can judge other people's foibles accurately. That's one reason why we are so fascinated by public apologies. Generally, they are inadequate and confirm "badness." On rare occasions, if they're convincing, they can flip the switch on our perception of a person from "bad" to "good."

Three years after Hulk Hogan was caught on tape making a racial tirade, he was returned to World Wrestling Entertainment's Hall of Fame, from which he'd been removed. WWE's statement said, "This second chance follows Hogan's numerous public apologies and volunteering to work with young people, where he is helping them learn from his mistake." Terry Bollea (his real name) said he's grateful for another chance, which he's been praying for. The public question that has arisen is whether he has done enough to prove that he's a changed man.[7]

Not only must a public apology demonstrate convincing contrition. It must also meet Step Four's requirement of preventing repetition. The most important aspects seem to me to be the same as those that hold between individuals. True regret and empathy do change your perspective, for sure, but is the change lasting? Will it be reflected in habits, circumstance, awareness, behavior?

For Annie, who'd been temporarily abandoned by her friend, accepting Margo's sincere regret wasn't hard, but thinking about the future made her uneasy. They both knew Margo might feel like "running away" again. With me, Margo identified alternative strategies for handling conflicts in the future: developing stress-management skills to prevent emotional flooding, that is, becoming overwhelmed by feelings that seem unmanageable; and bringing up small problems earlier, when they are more easily managed. Indeed, the next challenge soon arose for her: She and Annie were talking at lunch when Margo felt hurt and misunderstood. At first, she felt she had to leave the restaurant, but she returned after a few minutes and spoke directly about what had bothered her. Both women were happy that she had handled things differently. She had been able to change her way of responding. Together, they were completely capable of dealing with what had hurt her feelings.

Beyond changing her behavior, Margo wanted to understand better the roots of her defensive withdrawals, as well as their triggers. With me, she reviewed her emails to Annie and was surprised to see how "mean" they were. In her therapy, she discovered that her strong reaction to Annie's continued wish to be in touch could have been more related to Margo's mother's intrusiveness than it was to her friend's innocent attempts to reach her. The realization that she could be affected by "old movies" opened her perspective and led to still more curiosity. She will make mistakes in the future, as we all will, but she will probably not make these same ones.

Around the time of the confirmation hearings for now justice Brett Kavanaugh, people debated how responsible an adult should be for earlier, adolescent misbehavior. One essential factor seems to be whether there is evidence that the person has learned and changed since the past harm occurred. In the hearings, not only did Justice Kavanaugh not show that he as an adult had changed in attitude or approach from how he behaved as an adolescent, he also emphasized his ongoing attachment and commitment to the behaviors he engaged in long ago. He was remarkably combative in response to questions about his responsibility. In my *Cognoscenti* column of that time, I pictured an alternative reality that would have revealed maturity: "Can you imagine how different our view would be today if now-Justice Kavanaugh had said something like, 'I don't remember doing anything like that, but as a teenager and young man, I was often intoxicated and I did behave badly at times. I hope I didn't hurt you. But, if I did, I am deeply sorry for all the pain my awful behavior caused you.'"[8] Taking ownership of past mistakes is an important step in the process of assuring others that you have changed and intend to do better. Defensiveness and justification of past behavior say something else entirely.

When a self-defeating or harmful pattern comes to light, some form of soul-searching or greater self-awareness is often called for. The goal of greater self-knowledge is a common reason people seek psychotherapy, but mental health treatment isn't the only route. As we saw with James, whose wife had overworked, he benefited from meeting with a spiritual adviser. Sometimes the pair of people decide to work together—in or outside a therapy setting—to change a previous, unfortunate pattern.

Sarah, whose online cheating had hurt her boyfriend, Jonny, did go into therapy herself, because she didn't understand why she'd done what she'd done. She had always thought of herself as a good and honorable person, so it was disturbing and challenging to face that her actions had been anything but honorable. As she opened herself up to examining her assumptions and habits of thought, she became more aware of how she operated in the world. She learned to recognize her motivations and her defenses, which had previously been unclear to her. As she understood herself better, she realized she wanted to change more than this mistake about online infidelity. She believed that Jonny deserved the best she could be, but she also became invested in becoming self-responsible at a deeper level. During their time apart, she found more reason to trust herself and could promise Jonny a partner with more self-knowledge.

Kathryn Schulz, our "wrongology" expert, wrote that making errors isn't only a moral problem; "it is also a moral *solution*, an opportunity to rethink our relationship to ourselves, other people and the world."[9] That's what Sarah, Margo, and many others make of this kind of problem/solution. The recognition that you've hurt someone is fertile ground in which you have the chance to grow new strength, goodness, and a better future.

BUILD IN SYSTEMS TO
SUPPORT POSITIVE CHANGE

Pope Francis's responses to learning about clergy sexual abuse have ranged from earnest promises to expressions of sorrow to tone deafness. Clearly his good intentions have not been sufficient to effect complete change in the system. In April 2018, he invited Chilean victims of sexual mistreatment to his home to apologize for having voiced doubts about their accusations. He asked for their suggestions **"so these reprehensible facts never occur again."**[10]

Perhaps to his credit, he keeps returning to the subject. An entire year later, he issued a decree, "You Are the Light of the World," that outlined his thoughts for how to institute permanent and lasting change in the system that caused so much pain. In order to prevent sexual abuse and its cover-up from ever happening again, **"a continuous and profound conversion of hearts is needed, attested by concrete and effective actions that involve everyone in the Church."**

This sounds exactly like what we've been talking about here: people changing and their change being supported by external systems. Pope Francis proposed a new plan that requires the reporting of incidents of sexual abuse, including cover-ups; directs churches to establish submission systems for confidential complaints; sets a time limit for initial investigations; and protects those coming forward from retaliation. These rules incorporate sound ideas and model effective ways to reinforce change in a system.

Still, many victims and advocates worry that the plan lacks two major elements. The first issue is that the church will be policing itself, despite having fallen painfully short in the past. In a situation where so many people's trust has been shaken so badly, outside oversight might seem to be more trustworthy. Second, no sanctions were established for violations of the new rules. Without tangible consequences, it's less likely that the new policies will be followed.[11] We can hope that the pope will continue to return to this crucially important challenge, to strengthen this process with enforcement, and to demonstrate that the church is truly different in the future.

In personal relationships, repetition of hurtful actions makes it hard to know if a repair will "stick" or just be followed by the same disappointment. No one wants to be that partner who "screwed up *again*." Neither, of course, do you want to hurt or let down the person who is willing to try again with you. The question here for Step Four is: What will ensure that you will not make the same hurtful mistake again? You might think that good intentions will simply make it right, and in some cases they will—especially for small, recent habits. But most people don't change habits easily, permanently, without some structure to support them. I've seen wonderful people with great motivation insist that they don't need to set up any plan to support change. I don't mean to be discouraging, but I do mean to be realistic: Sometimes they come back, wiser and alone.

More often, though, I've witnessed pairs of people who create some form of a protective plan or system to support new habits, some ways to keep themselves together and moving forward. These strategies can include pursuing more self-understanding, asking for accountability partners, setting up administrative or scheduling routines, using technology to stay on track, establishing deliberate new communication routines, or creating follow-up systems to catch early signs of things going awry. You can schedule check-ins and adjust your plan if it doesn't work. You can let it evolve, as long as everyone stays focused on establishing a new, lasting path to trust.

Sometimes the hurtful habit is a relatively small thing that, when repeated, can grow into bigger hurt, as happened with Sam's lateness and Mario's missed toast for his aunt. Well before Aunt June's retirement party, Sam's casual approach to time commitments and his frequent tardiness had become a source of chronic frustration for Mario. The couple's moment of crisis and understanding led Sam to promise he would place greater value on his partner's family commitments. The men merged their electronic calendars so Sam could keep better track of their shared schedule. Although Mario believed his absentminded husband's good intentions and no longer felt angry, he doubted the electronic calendars would be enough.

Sam acknowledged that he's had a lifelong problem with distractibility and procrastination that's caused him serious problems before. "I'm just not ready to go get diagnosed and medicated for my ADD!"

Mario immediately replied, "Of course, that's only if and when you ever want to. But I know you hate me to nag you, and I don't know how else to get you to remember things."

I stepped in. "Nagging usually has the *opposite* of the intended effect." They both laughed.

I asked, "Sam, do you need reminders?"

He acknowledged, "I'm afraid so. But I tune him out when he tells me the same thing over and over."

Together they developed a system of limited, specific reminders from Mario (one reminder by voice and one by text), augmented by Sam's setting his own electronic alarm reminders. This "administrative solution" may not yet be perfect, but as a shared plan, it can be updated as needed. The most helpful part of this resolution is that the partners are on the same page, dealing with the same problem, rather than glaring at each other across a gulf of misunderstanding and helpless resentment.

As for Lisa and Philip, whose conflict and distance—left over from their wedding—had been longer-lasting and more serious, they approached their makeup wedding ceremony with some trepidation. They were aware of the huge costs the old, unmade apology had racked up. More than once, they stumbled back into bickering and retreated to their more cynical, mutually critical views of each other. We instituted changes in their communication habits, such as slowing down reactivity using the annoyingly tedious dialogue method mentioned earlier (Chapter 4)—so they could be mad at me instead of at each other. As they got better at recognizing their pattern of pointless arguments, they began to call their bickering the "picture-hanging syndrome," which helped them view it as a distinct habit they could challenge together. When one of them labeled what was going on as "picture hanging," it reminded them both of their alliance, that is, their shared desire to make a good relationship.

They both worried about getting off track again. Like an athlete recovering from an injury, a pair of people reconnecting after a relationship hurt has to use strategies to prevent reinjury.

Lisa fretted, "Getting 'remarried' really is a wonderful thing for us, but how can I be sure we won't get stuck again? I want to believe that you won't ignore my feelings and leave me alone."

Philip had already acknowledged his error of not taking her concern seriously and he vowed to remain more receptive. On the other hand, he worried that there could be another problem that Lisa might keep from him.

She agreed. "I can't believe I let this whole thing go on for so long and I didn't even realize I was doing it."

To prevent both old patterns, they established a low-pressure but regular time to check in with each other, at first every other week after work on Wednesdays—which had been the time of their appointments with me. Because they felt they could be most truthful in writing, each one would write the other a thoughtful letter before their regular check-ins.

Another way to think about their efforts to change their relationship habits is that they're a form of the "psychological safety" that we heard about earlier. In my practice and in my own marriage, I've witnessed that the agreement to keep coming back, to keep facing whatever needs facing, is a crucial element. If you want a good shot at fully repairing the hurt, you may need to return to the table until you get it right. That's because our understanding develops over time. We can't always put into words what's bothering us right away. Being willing to come back to the conversation, to ask again or try to speak again, gives you more chances to reach understanding and to change the story going forward.

Both large organizations and pairs of people can learn from the harms of the past. They can set up—and maintain—a better future, a changed reality that's stronger and more fair.

PRACTICE SCRIPTS FOR STEP FOUR

- "Here's how I will make sure this never happens again."

- "I want to do whatever I can to earn your trust again."

- "I promise to take responsibility for changing my routine/habits/mind-set."

- "Can we figure out a way together to change the way we do family communications?"

- "Will you please tell me if you see that we're sliding into the old pattern ['picture hanging'] again?"

- "I really want all this pain and challenge to make me and us better than we were before."

PART III

WHAT, THERE'S MORE?

CHAPTER 8

The Aftermath

The best aspect of a good apology is that everyone wins.

Almost universally, a sincere apology results in positive regard, rather than retribution or anger. Together, both—or all—parties can home in on compassionate accountability, rather than doubling down on their own sense of right and wrong. Everyone involved can get a fresh start.

We generally think of hurt feelings and big misunderstandings as bad things. But such disappointments are often necessary for the development of a sturdy relationship. Following a painful disappointment and real repair, something unique to the pair of people is born. This new relationship is an original creation, made by the people who mended the problem. Without mistakes—some of which are inevitable—people wouldn't have the chance to learn so much about each other or to build better ways of communicating. When you heal a relationship breach, you develop a better understanding of the other person, and you end up being more understood yourself. When all the steps are followed and the apology is accepted, there is a whole new set of possibilities.

I hadn't heard from Cathleen and Terry for fifteen years. Earlier in their marriage, they'd sought help dealing with the painful recovery from an affair. Immediately after Terry had found out about Cathleen's unfaithfulness, she had ended her extramarital relationship. At first, she'd been penitent, but over time she'd become frustrated with Terry's ongoing struggle to "get over" his painful reaction. In our first session, she had asked, "What more can I do? I've said I'm sorry a hundred times. It was a terrible mistake and I won't ever do anything like that again. But is this the way it's going to be from now on?"

Back then, both partners had wanted to stay together, but they weren't sure they could get past the betrayal of trust and resultant crisis in their relationship. They'd become chronically short-tempered with each other. They worried about the effect of their conflict and their potential separation on their adolescent children.

Cathleen loved her husband and deeply regretted her actions—especially how they'd hurt him—but the two of them were stuck in an incomplete apology. Together, they entered a challenging but shared process of reconciliation. As part of Step One, Terry helped Cathleen understand what he needed: primarily, patience and more invitation to talk with her about how this had affected him. They worked their way through the apology steps. Finally, in Step Four, preventing a repetition of the harm, they discovered that they had long ago fallen into self-defeating patterns when they communicated. For example, Terry rarely spoke up if he disagreed with his wife, and Cathleen rarely asked his opinion, especially in matters of the home and children. In fact, she knew very little about his views and carried the burden of raising their children on her own. Their worlds had become almost completely separate and distinct.

The Aftermath

That isolation from each other hadn't seemed important before, but as they engaged so intimately in their repair work, they became emotionally closer, more connected. Observing their relationship, we all recognized the fertile ground for problems this once-normal distance could again become. They wanted to prevent their old ways from driving them further apart again. So, together, they worked to change the way they communicated, which required considerable effort and several setbacks. They established time to "really talk" with each other, she made a point to remember to ask his opinion, and he worked to be clearer and more expressive. Habit change is very hard for everyone, but they kept at it, because, through the first three apology steps, they'd gained confidence in their ability to handle tough challenges.

What I see in relationships in which an effective repair has been made is not just that resentment, distance, and scorekeeping are reduced. Shared learning and mutual openness let light into previously opaque patterns or established habits of communication. The "old way" of being together is over, which is why well-known couples therapist Esther Perel is known to ask partners after the crisis of infidelity, "What do you want your *new relationship* to be like?" (Emphasis mine.) She wrote, "To repair is to re-pair."[1] A new relationship makes surprising things possible.

Years after they'd first come to see me, Cathleen and Terry returned to my office, seeking a consultation regarding a grandchild they were concerned about. As they explained the child's situation, they passed the narrative back and forth easily. It was like talking with a different couple from the one I'd first met. They had been taking care of the little girl two days a week, together, for the past year. Unlike the way they had functioned—so separately—when I'd first met them, it was clear that they now shared the pleasures and the authority of this childcare role. After we discussed the child's needs at length and what they could do for her, they wanted to fill me in on what this year of babysitting had been like for them.

Terry enthused, "I had no idea babies were so much fun. And so tiring." Then, more slowly: "It's been my first chance to raise a child with Cathleen, since I kind of missed it last time." When their children were young, they'd not been close teammates like they became after their reconciliation.

"And he's a natural, so loving and sweet with her." She mused, "But I don't think the two of us would have ever considered taking this on if we hadn't learned how to really connect with each other. Do you, Terry?"

He shook his head. "And think what we would have missed."

Many believe that a good relationship shouldn't encounter serious breaches like infidelity, but mutual trust can actually become much stronger after such a problem. A couple grows into its own unique strength as a result of healing together from hurt. If you can hang in—and keep returning to each other—with enough open-minded goodwill and respect, you become wiser about yourself and about your partner. You become more like the couple you want to be.

We're not aiming for perfection here, but for shared acceptance of what's true—which includes flaws and mistakes and hurts. The Japanese have developed an art form known as *kintsukuroi*, in which the cracks that remain after repairing broken pottery are lined with gold and silver, which creates something profoundly new and beautiful.

For example, Sarah and Jonny worked hard for months to repair their relationship because it was so important to both of them. As they mended their "cracks" and came back together, they shared their "mountain moment," which has remained a lovely reminder for them. When they find themselves in the midst of misunderstandings that seem to lead them down rabbit holes, they use the metaphor purposefully to evoke the wider perspective they found on that trip. They've created a way to recover the shining clarity about what's most important, which helps them get through and transform bad moments.

The Aftermath

*   *   *

Similarly, trust within work teams does not evolve as a result of being a conflict-free office; rather, it develops as everyone involved comes to trust conflict-resolution skills. That means in order to develop high-functioning teams, team members must experience and deal with conflict in a respectful manner.

Even in the case of parenting, an arena where people feel a lot of pressure to do things "right," it turns out to be crucially important for a child's development that the parent *isn't* perfect. Heinz Kohut, who developed self psychology, taught that "optimal frustration"—that is, tolerable disappointments, such as not being perfectly understood and responded to—is necessary for the development of a child's internal psychological structures. Similarly, pediatrician and psychoanalyst D. W. Winnicott described the "good-enough mother" as one who initially adapts closely to her infant's needs but then gradually begins to "fail." It's this "disillusionment" that enables the child to give up the fantasy of perfect union, which is necessary to develop a relationship to the real world.[2] A perfect mother is an impossibility, but a good-enough mother is a real person. Just so, a perfect relationship is an impossibility, and being stuck in that fantasy won't help you build a real relationship.

On all these fronts—a child's psychological development, a working team's success, and a relationship between two people—the process of breach followed by repair is not an unfortunate event and definitely doesn't have to signal the end of a relationship. On the contrary, it's necessary. The mending is what weaves the fabric of the future relationship. Even in a relationship full of frequent rifts and conflicts, as between a parent and an adolescent, the goal shouldn't be to prevent all the disconnections. As my wise therapist once told me, it's better to focus on learning to repair them better.

* * *

Prior to their earlier crisis and repair, neither Terry nor Cathleen would have anticipated how much they enjoyed being with each other. They'd previously lacked a sense of emotional partnership. When I saw them again after they'd had years to value it and each other, they acknowledged that the connection they now enjoyed had been hard-won. Terry characterized the crisis many years ago as "the best worst time" in their lives.

Cathleen underscored his message: "Yes, saving our marriage was definitely the hardest thing we've ever done—"

"But the most important one." Terry finished her sentence and added, "Except the kids, of course."

He continued, "We had no idea what we'd have to deal with since we saw you, what with teenagers and failing parents and our own medical problems."

"But, for us, it's been all about handling it together." Cathleen smiled at him before turning back to me.

I have seen so many couples experience this kind of upsurge of positive relationship esteem after going through a good apology together: "We did this really hard thing together and now we get to have a better relationship!"

Even more important, because they've learned to trust each other and their relationship, inevitable challenges in the future are less frightening. The couple now has shared vocabulary. They have mutual understanding about how to approach conflict and hardship. They have built skills to handle whatever rough spots they run into.

HOW APOLOGIES MAKE US BETTER

The process of bending and listening, the softening itself, is valuable. We've heard about how better connections with other people improve your physical health. In addition, a well-made apology enhances your spiritual well-being and potentially expands your range of humanness. In other words, by facing your own mistakes, you can find a greater sense of compassion for others'. In contrast, because Rolland couldn't open himself to this kind of self-examination, he not only lost a valuable connection, he missed an opportunity for this kind of expansiveness and growth.

Facing your own failure or error can make your understanding of other people's failings more complex. Rather than a morally simplistic view, you don't have to think of other people as either like you or unlike you. Sarah, who spent months working out amends with her boyfriend Jonny, began to change her perspective on many other aspects of her life. She'd been a sharp young prosecutor, keen to prove defendants at fault, but she gradually became more drawn toward understanding the people, especially young people, who'd been accused of crimes. Eventually, she switched sides to become a public defender in juvenile court instead. Sarah didn't imply any moral distinction between the two roles, both of which are necessary in our judicial system. Primarily, she said, the aspects of the cases that she got to spend time on seemed inherently more interesting and absorbing to her. But, too, she felt more sympathy about the kids' bad decisions than she used to and she valued the opportunity to contribute to someone's taking a better path.

By dealing directly with your responsibility to someone you've caused pain, you transform wrongdoing into an opportunity for positive change. In an essay about Lent, Rachel Howard wrote that the Christian forty-day period preceding Easter "disrobes" bad feelings, making them more evident. In stasis, guilt can become pathological, but during Lent—as in a good apology—wrongdoing has room to be examined and provides "narrative progression" for a person's guilt.[3] Facing a problem or atoning for a "sin" makes it possible to rewrite the story. A good apology provides a potential arc for that narrative.

When guilt is allowed to push you to make a relationship repair, it becomes transformed into self-respect. An example of such progression can be seen in the story of James and Mariah, the couple who had been stuck in a pattern of her harmful overworking. After he took all the apology steps, James's personal story changed. He no longer carried in his body that buildup of guilt ("silt guilt") that had left him feeling too overwhelmed to take effective action. He then could stand up with more self-respect and with much less shame. As humbling as it can be to face the fact that you've been wrong or done wrong, taking your lumps for imperfection—in a productive way—improves your outlook and, effectively, your character.

Your willingness to tackle good apologies can become an example for the people around you. For children in particular, learning about this transformation can have wonderful effects. They often have a natural sense of fairness, sometimes annoyingly so. A child can learn a parallel sense of empathy. If a young person can repair a hurt effectively, only good things follow: increased self-esteem, a more peaceful playroom/classroom/home, and deeper understanding about how our interdependent lives affect one another for good or ill. These elements form the basis for good relationships with other people. If a child can make things right when they've done something wrong or made a mistake that hurt someone, the experience is bone-deep. They internalize a model in which—as in restorative justice—everyone is treated with compassion rather than punishment, which is more likely to promote shame.

UNFINISHED BUSINESS

Influential educator Stephen Covey wrote, "If I were to summarize in one sentence the single most important principle I have learned in the field of interpersonal relations, it would be this: Seek first to understand, then to be understood."[4] That's the right order for our apologizer to follow, too.

Many conflicts between people are more complicated than a four-step model, used once, can fully resolve. Especially when the situations have been ongoing, there are usually hurts and complaints on both sides. I might hurt you unknowingly and you might react in a way that hurts me—which makes me feel that you are the cause of my pain, so I react negatively, and so on, over time. If things have become snarled into a tangle of reactions and counterreactions, it can be a dicey situation in which to offer an apology. For one thing, whose responsibility is it to go first? For another, in a troubled relationship, people often lack faith that they will get their "turns." How do you make it fair to everyone involved? If everyone feels hurt, no one may be inclined to apologize. But if one brave and humble person is willing to offer a sincere apology, you have a way to begin the healing that's needed.

If you are the one taking the first step toward making an apology—regardless of how hurt or angry you are about something the other person did—you must set your own need for an apology aside, temporarily. That's much harder than it might sound. It requires remembering that the point here is to do what you can do to restore your relationship, while keeping track of your needs, too. It's only after the first round of the apology process (all four steps) that you get to bring up your own grievance. At that point, roles are exchanged, and the person previously in the role of injured party becomes the apologizer and has to inquire and listen, and so on. We're talking about taking turns, so that everyone's hurt is dealt with. The first apology is not always the final, tidy resolution; rather, it can be just the first round, the beginning of an ongoing conversation—or one that can be reopened when needed.

For example, after Monique, whose family learned to include her husband Desmond, had completed all the apology steps sincerely, there remained a sore place in her feelings. She realized that she was upset with Desmond for how he'd handled his complaints. Over the few years they'd been together, he seemed to have brought up problems often when she was under immediate pressure, especially parenting stress. She replayed some of those times in her mind and became quite angry at him. It seemed to her that this habit had made it much harder for her to deal with his concerns and caused her always to feel torn between allegiances. Unaware of its effect on her, Desmond started to tell her about a small issue with one of the kids while she was juggling dinner preparation and trying to organize by phone the kids' rides for the week. She initially reacted with anger but, to her credit, recognized an opportunity to use the skills they'd practiced with me. She told him she wanted to set aside a time to talk in the next day or so.

By the time they sat on the porch the next evening, Monique had settled down and was able to confront him in a serious but calm voice. First, she told him she wanted him to listen to her explain something she was upset with him about. Desmond later told me that he didn't feel defensive at first. He listened willingly, until she characterized him as seeking out the worst times to talk to her. He objected and she backed off. "You're right. I'll try to talk only about the effect you've had on me, like we did in Molly's office."

Together they slowed down the process. She spoke directly and he listened carefully. Desmond could address his mistake with sincere regret, because he decidedly did not want to make her feel torn or overwhelmed. They talked further about how he could make it up to her and how to set reminders in place so he didn't do it again. I heard about this only when they came in for another appointment a couple of years later, because of a shared problem with their extended families. They'd managed the whole thing with what they'd learned by going through the apology process so thoroughly when Desmond had needed the earlier apology. Monique told me how much she appreciated her husband's willingness to change his habit and how much better things worked for them because of it.

Another illustration arose in Margo's friendship with Annie. You may recall that Margo had initially held her silence about her own hurt feelings for too long—which had led her to abruptly cut off the relationship. Annie knew there'd been earlier, unaddressed problems, so, after her hurt had substantially healed, she turned the tables and asked Margo to help her understand how she, Annie, had hurt her. This was her Step One. For Margo, telling her friend the truth about her hurt was even harder than it had been to ask about Annie's. She needed encouragement both because self-revelation went against her habit and because she still felt bad about having hurt her friend. But eventually Annie convinced her that she really wanted to know. Margo did her best and they proceeded with the next three steps, this time in the other direction.

Oprah Winfrey, a highly influential public figure, demonstrated a different kind of unfinished business that can come up for the "injured party." In 2006, she'd demanded an on-air apology from James Frey. She'd endorsed his memoir, even calling in with support to Larry King's interview show when the veracity of the stories was questioned. But when she learned that he had deceived "every single reader," that he was "the man who conned Oprah," she asked him back onto her show and sternly held him to account.

However, the angry, uncompassionate way she'd spoken to him on her show bothered her. A couple of years later, she called him to offer a personal apology, because she'd violated her own values. Specifically, she is committed to getting to the truth of what people have to say, but her anger had prevented her from hearing his side at all. In her statement of regret, she made it clear to him and to her vast following that she needed to make amends because she didn't behave the way she believes she should. Hers is a great example of someone making a humble self-assessment and taking responsibility for her actions. To her wide audience, she contributes a model that others can follow after their own situations have become more complex than solely the initial injury.[5]

Another kind of unfinished emotional business sometimes affects the person who caused harm. In the field of medical injuries, a controversial term—"second victim"—has been applied to the physician who's suffering because of the harm he or she caused to a patient. Hurting someone you're supposed to be helping, of course, deeply troubles the would-be healer or helper. In any circumstance—whether a medical error or a relationship mistake—the primary obligation is to address the needs of the person hurt by your actions.

But, in my experience, the person who inflicted hurt also needs compassion. For those of you reading this book because you want to make amends, remember that you personally fare much better and are left with less corrosive guilt if you can make a thorough apology to the one you hurt. For both parties in a personal conflict, it may help you to bear in mind that repairing a relationship ultimately requires you to find compassion for the other, as well as for yourself.

HEALING EFFECTS ON THE COMMUNITY

When you harm one person, it can affect others—family members, community members, friends. Writer Cris Beam holds that "the truth is, an apology is rarely a private event between two people: When you harm one person, you harm many." If, as she writes, an intimate relationship injury can "scatter scars," she goes on to "hope that an intimate apology, made public, can heal them."[6] That's precisely why restorative justice programs involve neighbors, community members, and family members of both the victim and the offender.

The Aftermath

As an individual, you can also affect the larger community directly with your apology steps, as did the veterans who helped restore communities after causing harm to other communities. Aaron Pratt Shepherd, whose writing about moral injury we discussed in Chapter 6, said that deeds of atonement are not meant to "win forgiveness but to enrich the life of the betrayed community." He quoted nineteenth-century philosopher Josiah Royce as saying that the repair "shall be so wise and rich in its efficacy that the spiritual world, after the atoning deed, shall be better, richer, more triumphant amidst all its irrevocable tragedies than it was before."[7]

The high-flown language may not appeal to you, but your public apology can nonetheless become a model for other people who need to see how it can be done well. For example, Dan Harmon, the television showrunner who issued a thorough YouTube apology, implored other men to think differently about how they treat women. In my *Cognoscenti* column, I asked former vice president Joe Biden to make a good apology to Anita Hill, so that it could be a model for other men. Frequently, people send me stories of amends, excited to share accounts of sound apologies. I believe we are moved by them because they show us how we can all do better.

We are especially hungry for these models in the current climate of divisive, ugly discourse and the factors that contribute to it. A few commentators have written about how to change that reality. For example, conservative commentator Arthur C. Brooks recently commented that the contempt we feel for those who disagree with us is a virulent element of today's culture that we should change. He said, "What we need is not to disagree less, but to disagree better."[8]

Michael Gulker, who teaches Christian church leaders to deal better with conflict, agreed. He described how we tend to approach interpersonal gatherings "as Democrats or Republicans, liberals or conservatives, feminists or traditionalists, religious people or nonbelievers." He went on to underscore how people anticipate—inaccurately—that they already know from mass media what the "other side" is like, "that anyone who disagrees with me is either uneducated, stupid or evil."[9] Listening to one another with respect and speaking honestly are not only what you have to do with people you know in order to have favorable outcomes; those two habits also form one of the bases on which democracy was built. The presence of more than one voice or perspective acts to curtail the most dangerous errors we might make as a society.[10] But the resulting conflict can be resolved only when various sides listen to one another and acknowledge that we are not essentially enemies. We are people with some different perspectives, needs, and interests.

I don't mean to imply that all political disagreements can be resolved by communicating with my steps, but I do believe they help. What would be different if you approach the other person with curiosity and respect, setting aside your own opinions for a moment? Or if your goal is establishing (or reestablishing) trust in the relationship? Or if you can be both confident and humble enough about your own positions that you are open to understanding someone else's? Resolution is not about relinquishing your own beliefs; it's about learning what's at the root of someone else's position so that you can better understand them—and potentially the overlap of your interests. For someone else to be right, you don't have to be wrong. Sometimes, for example, what hurts someone isn't that you say or do anything "wrong," per se, but that your message or action is based on an incomplete understanding of them. It's my belief that everyone benefits from the richness of wider understanding and from including more people's voices in a resolution.

One of my favorite communication rules is "When it's your turn, you may speak as if you're right, but you must listen as if you're wrong." Again, it's not easy to do, but it's a worthwhile aspiration.

At times, we all tend to listen only long enough to see if the other person agrees with us, or to prepare our response. However, the basic rules of good listening are widely available and pretty clear: Temporarily suspend or hold in abeyance your point. Calm yourself enough to focus on the other person's message. Take time to understand it as well as you can, which may mean asking follow-up questions. Resist the urge to try to "fix" the problem. Try to empathize with the other person's point of view. These are all aspects of Step One in a good apology. If you want to contribute to more mutually respectful public discourse—and personal relationships—you must listen at least as well as you speak.

THE FULL IMPACT TAKES TIME

Patience is especially relevant *after* an apology has been undertaken. For one thing, it takes time to see what really happens next. Have things actually improved? Are some aspects of the resolution working better than others? Has everyone followed through with putting the change into practice? Many changes take time to become real.

My colleague Susan Fairchild, a therapist and meditation teacher, told me about an apology that was just the *beginning* of a profound change, which continued to evolve across time. At a self-compassion workshop led by a well-known mindfulness teacher, Christopher Germer, she was troubled by the way he presented an idea. As she and many other students, mostly female, had sat surrounded by portraits of white men, Dr. Germer had mentioned the issue of marginalization but, as she pointed out to him, had neglected to identify gender as a relevant basis for marginalization in the culture—and in the room. He heard her out (Step One), told her he was really sorry (Step Two), and addressed the issue directly and compassionately on his return to the workshop. In the following months, he and his colleagues changed the curriculum of their teacher training to reflect the way culturally influenced and trauma-induced shame can affect the body, particularly for a woman (Step Three).

Two years later, when Ms. Fairchild facilitated a workshop with Dr. Germer, she witnessed an impressive example of his having changed. He talked to the group about shame that becomes embodied and he led them in an exercise in which they physically used their arms to push away messages that limit them, while shouting "No!" His gracious and responsible apology, in response to her earlier feedback, continues across time (Step Four).[11]

As Michael Gulker, who helps religious leaders manage conflict, has said about learning to face conflict directly, "It's a long game." He trains people to communicate with those who differ from them on any number of dimensions. In his workshops, people learn to discuss disagreements, including political ones, because we "need to learn to live together." It takes time to build relationships, so "if you're going to engage someone you disagree with over time, you have to cultivate things like patience, humility, gentleness and forbearance," which are less necessary if you talk only with people you already agree with. He measures the success of his work by the fact that those he's trained continue to train others and to request more material and further training.[12] As people learn the value of such brave communication, they appear to discover that disagreements and conflicts don't have to be seen as roadblocks to be avoided, but instead as tools for understanding one another better.

Large, societal wrongs may not be repaired during our lifetimes, but there are many who argue that that shouldn't stop us from moving the process along as much as we can. To be sure, incremental progress over time is harder to see and, for many, harder to value. But the immense benefits of making mistakes, failing, and then trying again may finally be entering the public domain. For example, Silicon Valley's wildly innovative climate is said to be infused with a "Fail fast, fail often" maxim. This resembles the way a young child develops new capacities, by way of trial and error, which leads to crucial learning.[13] In recent years, Stanford University's Resilience Project has focused on ways to support students through their inevitable failures. The Resilience Project regularly hosts a program called "Stanford, I Screwed Up," which celebrates students' "epic failures." The project's goal is to "change the perception of failure from something to be avoided at all costs, to something that has meaning" and provides great opportunities to learn.[14]

This is distinctly different from how, historically, most Americans have been taught to solve problems. Illustrating this point are findings from a landmark 1994 study that investigated why the lowest-scoring math class in Japan outscored the highest-scoring American classroom. It turns out that young students in Japan kept at their math problems, despite multiple wrong answers, until they solved them. In contrast, American students aren't likely to keep trying if they don't succeed quickly. The authors reported that, in the United States, mistakes are considered psychologically very costly. Further, many American parents and teachers believe that mathematical ability is innate, which makes trying again less relevant.[15] In many cases, recovery, change, and growth are not viewed as possible. Therefore students are less likely to try again, much less learn new ways to solve problems.

Any step-by-step efforts, or trying again and again, take time. Harkening back to cultural norms introduced earlier, we find yet another way the model of confident certainty doesn't act in our best interests: It makes us less able to work at problems that take time, patience, and humility—endeavors like communicating through conflict and apologizing.

SAVING VERSUS WASTE

Good apologies give us a way to preserve, even strengthen, our connections. Shared history doesn't have to be interrupted, nor relationships lost.

A Good Apology

Like many people, you may have longed for simpler, more perfect understanding between yourself and the people you love. When that sense is challenged by communication mishaps or hurt feelings, your happy relationship picture is shattered. Fortunately, a good apology can mend your relationship in a way that makes it stronger, and wonderful in a different way. Like the Japanese *kintsukuroi* pottery, with cracks lined in precious metals, restored wholeness has its own loveliness. The mending metaphor from my childhood continues to resonate for me. Among the tiny, discarded objects I collected when I was young, a sky-blue, glued-back-together pitcher became my favorite vase. I liked to trace the crack lines with my fingers and my eyes. They showed the history of its repair, how it was made whole again.

People who've healed a hurt together have created a new basis for relationship, a more reciprocal pattern for facing future challenges. With an effective way to repair hurt, what you get instead of the tidy, unrealistic image is a more complicated but more satisfying truth.

AFTER THE APOLOGY

- **Positive effects on a relationship**

- **Positive effects on the one who apologizes**

- **Positive effects on the recipient of the apology**

- **Resolving unfinished business**

- **Healing effects on the community**

- **Full impact in time**

- **Preserving versus wasting**

CHAPTER 9

What About the Apology Recipient?

If you've been hurt, it is in no way your sole responsibility to repair your own hurt, but you may want to influence how an apology goes. How can you ask for and guide an apology so it will be genuinely satisfying and healing? How can you decide whether or not to accept an apology at all?

You have the power to help others understand how you have been affected by their actions. You do not need to wait for someone to "come around," "take responsibility," or "realize what they've done" on their own. Together you can create a unique process. Depending on the relationship, it may behoove you to tell the full truth, until it's all out. This radical, loving honesty pays off in mutual, intimate knowledge.

Allie, an intelligent and well-liked sixteen-year-old, had come to therapy because of anger and depression following their parents' divorce. (Allie identifies as gender-fluid.) One day, they arrived in my office with a fresh "problem that isn't really a problem." While they were out of town for a family funeral, their boyfriend, Devin, had kissed a girl at a party. But, because he'd called right away and confessed, they'd already forgiven him.

"He still wants to talk about it, but I don't want him to feel bad. And it's really okay. I know he's sorry, so I told him we didn't need to talk about it anymore."

We sat for a moment and they rolled their eyes. "You probably think I should talk about it more, right?"

If a loved one approaches you to begin an apology, you might be tempted to accept it before it's complete, whether because you appreciate the other person's effort and sincerity, because you want to let them off the hook, or because you are uncomfortable with the whole thing. But your relationship is better served by patience with the process, including the time it takes to know what you need.

"Well, if that would help, sure. Want to tell me any more about what this is like for you?"

They were quiet while they sorted out mixed feelings. "I know he loves me and he feels bad about what happened. Isn't that enough?"

"It could be. Does that feel true to you?"

"Ugh. I probably wouldn't be talking about it now if it was really done. But you know what else? He seemed even more upset when I forgave him—which is just weird."

"We can talk about his feelings, too, if you want, but first I think we should understand how you feel."

As they sat with me, their eyes reddened and a tear slid down their cheek. They wiped it away with the back of their hand and began to talk about how they wanted their relationship with Devin, which has always been "so great," to be perfect—especially not like their parents'. They wanted "this whole kissing thing to just be over," so they wouldn't have to think about it.

"That's an understandable wish for sure, but it seems likely that ignoring it won't make it go away. You do have feelings about this." I encouraged them to take whatever time they needed to sort out their reactions and to decide if and when they wanted to continue the conversation with him.

"Here's the thing: I really, really, *really* don't want to make him feel worse! He's been so good about listening to me every time I need to talk about my crazy parents." Their eyes downcast, they lapsed into silence.

Allie's interest in protecting Devin's feelings was partly a kind impulse. They didn't want him to suffer unnecessarily. However, they also didn't have much experience dealing directly and successfully with uncomfortable feelings and wanted to avoid venturing into that territory of uncertainty. For the cultural and neuroscientific reasons discussed in Chapter 2, most of us prefer a quick and certain conclusion. Allie was no exception.

"You know, I think your relationship with Devin is strong enough that he might actually *want* to hear about your reactions." We paused while Allie took in that idea. I continued, "What do you think that kind of sharing would do for you two?"

Bravely, Allie reopened the subject with him. Apparently, Devin hadn't known what to do next, but he'd felt that his apology wasn't complete. Together, they talked at length. Allie asked him some hard questions and he asked them how he could earn their trust back. After a couple of difficult, emotional conversations, they felt much closer to each other.

When you've been hurt by someone, you have a wide range of choices. At the time, that may not be apparent. Heretofore, we've addressed the reasons a person might avoid *making* an apology, but we haven't yet considered why someone might avoid asking for an apology or might not want to accept one that's offered. To fully mend a relationship, the apologizer must take crucial steps, but the injured person has important roles to consider in this process as well.

ASK FOR THE APOLOGY YOU NEED—OR NOT

The most likely way you will ever receive a good apology is by asking for it. As we've seen, most people are apt to overlook their own mistakes and will resist facing them. Unless you tell them, they might not know how they've affected you. Within your relationship, you may need to initiate by telling the other person that you're hurt, upset, or angry and you want them to address the problem. It may seem straightforward, but it could be almost as hard as making the apology itself, for several reasons.

You don't like conflict. Ah yes, the overarching wish to avoid any unpleasantness can keep you from opening a conversation about the hurt you feel. The same complications, drawbacks, and advantages exist here as they do for the potential apologizer.

You don't trust the other person. The one who hurt you may not seem able to do what an apology takes. You lack faith in their ability to deal with the necessary steps or the extent to which they care.

You don't trust yourself. You doubt your own feelings, and/or aren't sure your experience of what happened is accurate. You may not believe that you deserve someone's effort to make amends for something that's hurt you.

You don't trust the relationship. Either because it's too new or because you've avoided facing problems, you have little experience dealing with hard things together. Or perhaps you are in a relationship

201

where you do not have equal power or legitimacy to bring up something that will challenge the other person.

Discussing problems also runs counter to the model of romantic love we have learned from movies and fairy tales, wherein two lovestruck people instantly become one pair of soul mates, with no mistakes or misunderstandings in the happily ever after.

<u>You don't trust that things can change</u>. Old roles, including ones you played in your original family, sometimes get a powerful hold on you. You may believe that you are doomed to continue in familiar patterns. Just as we've talked about how hard it can be to change a potential apologizer's habitual stance, your habits are stubborn, too. Asking for an apology may be a completely different script than you grew up with or than you've spoken before. To change requires not only that you "retrain" yourself to ask for what you need, but also that you develop faith that your relationship can change. The only reasons to work that hard are that you really want this relationship and that you want it to be as good as it can be.

ACCEPT THE APOLOGY OFFERED—OR NOT

Remember that the offer to make amends is always an invitation, not a demand. Although you may often want to, there is no obligation to accept an apology or even participate in the conversation. The one who wishes to make something right enters the process because he or she wants to address emotional guilt or moral pain—as well as to help you, the injured one, heal. It's the right thing for that person, but you, the recipient, might not feel the same way.

<u>Don't accept an apology too soon</u>. Of course, there are also times when you just aren't ready for an apology yet. In an ongoing relation-

ship, if you're too angry or raw to accept a loved one's amends, it pays to leave the door explicitly open for future repair opportunities. ("I'm not ready to talk about this right now, but I will want to at some point. Will you try again tomorrow?")

The mistake of forgiving too soon or too lightly, as Allie initially did after their boyfriend's kissing confession, can lead to an unfortunate pattern in which the hurt isn't really repaired. It can leave one or both people feeling as though there is unresolved business, uncertain about whether any further amends are called for. In these instances, the hurt stays present under the surface. Then, whenever the next hurt inevitably arises, both people are surprised by a larger reaction than the current injury calls for. This is a common reason couples consider therapy: Large reactions to apparently small mistakes confuse everyone. Remember how Lisa and Philip (whose wedding was marred by doubt and avoidance) found themselves in repetitive, pointless disagreements? Also, an incomplete repair functions like one that's been missed entirely. Until it's resolved, the air isn't really clear.

The question of trust. A profound reason not to accept an apology offer is if you don't believe the person is sincere. If you don't trust the person at all, you mustn't engage in the repair process by revealing any vulnerable feelings. On the other hand, if you think the person is probably trustworthy, this process is a pretty good testing ground. Taking the risk to trust a bit can reveal whether or not it's deserved; depending on how it goes, your trust grows or diminishes.

For many reasons, you might want to accept. When you receive or witness another person's sincere apology, you might feel receptive and want to accept it with the attitude of compassionate accountability. That is, you know the wrong is real, but you also believe in the redemptive possibility of making things right. In response to doctors' acknowledgments of mistakes, for example, medical patients feel "heard" and no longer vengeful. In response to Mr. Netanyahu's telephoned apology to Turkey, the door to resuming normal diplomatic relations was opened between two quarreling states. On very different levels, these events are good news for everyone involved.

SHAPE THE APOLOGY—OR NOT

It's critical to determine your particular timing needs: the time at which you're ready to begin the conversation, the time it takes you to respond, the time you need to become aware of what you want from the other person, and the time it takes you to be ready to move on from the problem—if that turns out to be possible. Even after a good apology has been undertaken, recovering from hurt can take time. In some circumstances, you encounter information that's new to you. You may need time to absorb the news, to consider what it means to you, and to discuss it further.

If you see that the other person is taking a risk by beginning an apology, you may want to embrace their effort. But it's important for you to take as long as you need. Ask for patience. You may need to sit with the apology for a while in order to discern if you need anything else. This is what happened with Sarah and Jonny, the couple for whom it took months to work through their breach of trust. Throughout most of the process, Jonny believed that the relationship was salvageable, and he had faith that he would probably be ready at some point to "get past it" and to trust her again. He just had no way of predicting how long that would take. While Sarah was learning about herself, he engaged in a similar effort, learning to pay attention to how he really felt and what he needed. It was hard for him to stick to his guns and to keep them both waiting while he went over the same worries and feelings and asked her innumerable questions. Now, they agree it was worth the time and struggle, that complete resolution takes time and exploration to develop.

For a relationship apology to work, it ultimately has to be a two-person event: The recipient, an active participant, receives and shapes the apology. For example, "Now I can see that you really understand how this hurt me"; "How can I be sure you won't do it again?"

In restorative justice programs, the victim or "affected party" is always involved from the beginning. In fact, this extrajudicial process doesn't take place at all unless the victim is amenable. The person who's been harmed may elect to participate to any degree desired and, if they don't want to attend in person, may send a proxy or a statement to be read to the opening circle. The affected party has the power to shape the process, not only in terms of presenting their side of what happened and its impact, but also in determining what requirements the offender must meet. The questions are: What would restore the victim to whole-ness? What must the responsible party do to make this wrong right?

These are parallel questions you can ask regarding personal hurts: What would restore you to wholeness? How can the other person make this wrong right?

Sometimes it's hard to know what you need from someone who's hurt you. Let me tell you about one of my favorite exercises. It begins with a person who's hurt. If you haven't received an apology you need, you may try this, too. Write a letter containing the message you wish your partner (or another important person) would write to you. Imagine what would help to heal the hurt you feel. Try to think through everything that you believe ought to be said and done in order to find resolution. By focusing on this question, you often discover most of what you need.

If you want to share it, your letter can be incredibly informative to your potential apologizer. By writing in detail what you need, you can help the other person to suspend their own perspective in order to understand yours. You also give them the space to process your experience when they're not in the heat of the moment with you. You're teaching the other person to do what Katherine Schulz, our "wrongology" expert from Chapter 2, recommends: Attend to counterevidence.

A new book, *The Apology*, by well-known feminist Eve Ensler, is written in the form of such a letter from her father. Although he's been dead for thirty years, it's the apology she needed him to make for physically and sexually abusing her during her childhood. She believes it can be a model for men who should apologize for mistreating women and can be healing for other women who've been victimized. Indeed, I think it could be, and it also demonstrates the potential therapeutic value of this exercise.[1]

CHANGE THE FUTURE OF YOUR RELATIONSHIP—OR NOT

Most of us lack the public platform Ms. Ensler uses to such remarkable effect, nor do we all have a public message like the one she is bringing to the world. What you may have is a relationship that has suffered, and, if you're lucky, someone has made an effort to heal the hurt. Following an apology, you want to prevent future hurt. Here are a few rules of thumb that may help.

Remember that fairy tales are misleading. Even Snow White and Prince Charming, if they have a lasting relationship, may have had to address his jealous feelings about the seven dwarves. At times, all relationships require work.

As with an automobile, apologies are repairs and you sometimes need maintenance to keep things running well. You and your partner may want to change your automatic reactions to problematic feelings that arise from time to time. Instead of impediments, think of them as opportunities to improve the health of your relationship's engine. Perhaps the best "ever after" couples are those who continue to be honest, vulnerable, and willing to repair misunderstandings.

Start as you mean to continue. Like many people, you may put your best—that is, most accepting and agreeable—foot forward in the beginning of a relationship. The risk therein is that you misinform the other person about what's actually okay or good for you. The mistake of letting too many small misdeeds go unchallenged creates a bad pattern that's harder to break. It behooves you to know yourself and what you can comfortably tolerate versus what will drive you crazy or make you feel bad. You are teaching your partner or friend how to treat you.

Unfortunately, this beginning-relationship pattern sometimes resets following a crisis and resolution, when both people feel tender and relieved. It may feel unnatural to communicate preferences when you're just grateful that you're no longer fighting, but you must—or you could be setting up the next problem. In Chapter 5, we saw that Desmond did not stop sharing his concerns with his wife, Monique, after her initial statement of regret. Even though they'd found a moment of resolution, his continued effort to address their problems was necessary in order to reach real and thorough understanding with her.

Clarity is kindness. Nice people spend a lot of time trying not to hurt anyone. Often that involves avoiding the truth or keeping things unclear. Sometimes, you might put off informing someone of an uncomfortable or complicated reality. You think that it's out of kindness, and maybe it is, but when the other shoe drops, that is, the person figures it out or you *have* to tell them, it usually hurts more. They ask, "Why didn't you tell me?" and you say, "I didn't want to hurt you."

Being clear is not necessarily unkind. Of course, it could be, but it's worth practicing to become better at presenting the truth in a kind way. This is also a social justice truism: Be brave enough to be clear and truthful. Direct communication can prevent later, worse hurt, as well as many kinds of misunderstandings.

FORGIVE—OR NOT

Just as you are not required to accept an apology at all, you are not required to forgive someone who's hurt you. A person may owe you an apology, but you don't owe them forgiveness.

Forgiveness is a huge and popular topic, written about by many insightful philosophers and psychologists who are far better informed than I am on this subject. I'm not attempting to make a thorough analysis of forgiveness in this book. But here is the most important message I've gathered on this topic: Forgiving someone who's harmed you may help them or the community, but the biggest beneficiary of your forgiveness often is you.

Exercising forgiveness lowers blood pressure, heart rate, and the amount of cortisol (a stress hormone) released into the system. A better-functioning immune system leads to better overall health and reduced risk of cardiovascular events. On the other hand, excess cortisol, which accompanies holding a grudge, is associated with all kinds of medical problems, the same ones that any chronic stress seems to cause.[2]

The Stanford Forgiveness Project has found that "skills-based forgiveness training" can reduce stress and physical health symptoms, including improved immune system functioning. Dr. Frederic Luskin, founder of the project, says that forgiveness is a learnable skill—consisting of steps that include self-care, stress management, and changing perspective—and that it just takes practice.[3]

For many people, religious faith requires them to forgive (or try to forgive) someone who's caused harm. For example, Asma Jama was assaulted by a fellow restaurant patron who heard her speaking Swahili to her family. The woman smashed a beer mug into Ms. Jama's face, causing substantial injury, which was followed by severe anxiety. Fourteen months later, in the courtroom, a visibly scarred Ms. Jama, who is Muslim, said, "My religion teaches me to forgive, so I can move on with my life. If I hold a grudge and I hold the hate against you, it's not going to serve me well." She expressed her wish that her assailant might learn something from the experience. Despite there being no evidence of remorse or change in her attacker, Ms. Jama has found new purpose in her own life as a supporter of other people's rights.

Similarly, after a white man murdered nine black churchgoers in Charleston, South Carolina, some of the survivors told him that they forgave him. One woman, Bethane Middleton-Brown, whose sister DePayne Middleton Doctor was killed in the mass shooting, said her sister had taught her that "we are the family that love built. We have no room for hating, so we have to forgive."[4] The bereaved Ms. Middleton-Brown gave us a strong example of what's become familiar reasoning, that to hate him would mean surrendering something else to a person who'd already taken so much from her and her family.

Faith led both women to forgive someone with whom they did not have a personal relationship, someone who had caused them enormous suffering. They actively chose to move through their experiences and seek out a new way to live in peace. To the extent that they could, they both chose to live without hate, which is in the best interest of their spiritual—and probably physical—health.

Freeing yourself from resentments and past harms can be a frankly spiritual discipline. The English poet Alexander Pope gave us the iconic line "To err is human; to forgive, divine." In his poem, he suggested that this capacity to forgive is aspirational, that we should try to be like the forgiving God and show mercy to humans who make mistakes.[5] Christians try to follow Jesus's dictum to turn the other cheek rather than respond to harm with a counterattack. During the

High Holidays Jews find ways to forgive people who've hurt them across the previous year and to let go of any grudges. If you can't work things out with the other person, at the end of the day, how you handle your injuries and hurts sometimes turns out to be between you and your higher self or between you and your God.

Anne Lamott wrote a pithy analogy that "not forgiving is like drinking rat poison and then waiting for the rat to die."[6] After challenging her own resistance to the idea of forgiveness as a positive thing, columnist Renée Graham called it an act of "strength and grace," even of defiance, because it claims your humanity in an inhumane circumstance.[7] It is when a person faces terrible loss or harm that we can see the powerful impact of forgiveness on them and the other people around them.

In the moving CNN documentary series *Redemption Project*, created by journalist Van Jones, perpetrators and victims of serious crimes come together to try to find peace. As one prisoner wept with remorse for having killed a teenage girl, the victim's father was moved to point out how important it was that the murderer had grown and changed in the twenty years since his crime. With great heart, he said, "It ain't where you start, it's where you finish."[8]

Recognition of this crucial aspect of human character is essential both to make a good apology and to forgive someone: We are not frozen forever at our worst moments, nor are we stuck always in our most painful times. A quotation by businessman and writer Paul Boese captures the possibility inherent in this truth: "Forgiveness does not change the past, but it does enlarge the future."[9]

There is not a right or wrong answer about whether you should forgive someone else. In my view, there is no morally superior way to handle this issue. It's up to you to do whatever will best aid your recovery from harm. If your particular harm is an echo of a larger societal problem, like harm to worshippers in a black church, congregants in a temple, or a mosque's faithful, you may face a different choice than someone who's dealing with purely personal hurt. As I write this book, the incidence of harm to people because of religious, racial, or ethnic identities appears to be on the rise in the United States. Public statements of forgiveness for a particular harmdoer may give the impression that the harm is healed, which could in turn provide the public with permission to stop thinking about it. On the contrary, you might think it's valuable for harm to be remembered. In these cases, dealing with the loss of a loved one becomes an important social justice issue, as well as an occasion of personal pain—which complicates the meaning of forgiveness.

GO FOR VENGEANCE—OR NOT

After someone hurts you, the urge to seek revenge is understandable. It's just as natural and perennial as it is to have the grace and strength to forgive and, especially in the beginning, comes more easily. You may want the person to be punished, to suffer because you've suffered. Certainly, most criminal justice models seem to serve the primary purpose of punishment, rather than healing for the victim or protection of the public.

One recent research finding may shed light on the meaning of punishment in the eyes of those who've been hurt. When a business has caused someone harm, not only do the customers want an apology; they want an action that costs the business something. A *Freakonomics* podcast presented the results of a large study of Uber customers who experienced a late arrival. An emailed apology after the negative experience had little effect on customers' future Uber spending. When the apology was accompanied by a promotional coupon toward a future ride, customers apparently found the apology more convincing—that is, the restitution had weight. Promotional coupons themselves, independent of an apology, were not effective in increasing spending.[10]

For me, this research raises the issue of punishment in general. If someone has hurt you, do you want them to be *hurt* in return or just to be *cost* something? What is the difference?

As we've heard, victims of crimes often do not want the maximum sentence for the perpetrators. They want a serious consequence, but they want it to make sense and to restore some balance for the hurt person(s) and the community.

In a striking example of supporting a less harsh punishment for someone who caused harm, a young woman who had been sexually assaulted supported a plea bargain that would let her assailant avoid prison time. The judge in the case was "baffled" because the charges were serious and the case was strong. But the young woman said she believes that everyone deserves a second chance. Making the process fit what she needed for her personal healing, she requested a different, specific consequence for him: a public apology in open court. In addition to other penalties, her harmdoer was ordered to "own up" and say exactly what he had done to her.[11] In court, she also told him, "I ask you to make your future untainted. I ask that you make a positive impact in every life you touch because the impact you made in mine and in my family's is enough for a lifetime." With evident emotion, he did indeed describe, in graphic detail, his "inexcusable behavior that night." He spoke further to the court: "She's incredibly courageous and it breaks my heart that I'm responsible for this. I feel deep, deep shame for having caused [the survivor] to go through this."[12]

Rather than imposing punishments, wise parents have long used natural consequences (allowing unfavorable outcomes that follow misbehavior) and restorative approaches (teaching the child to make restitution or restore what was broken), in order to help their children learn right from wrong. In behavioral mental health treatment designed to increase a desired behavior, a schedule of positive reinforcement is much more likely to be recommended than punishment. Punishment is less effective for changing human behavior, particularly in the long run.

YOU MAY GO FIRST—OR NOT

The most likely path to reconnection is for someone to step forward and take responsibility for whatever they've done that hurt the other. This, you may recall, is what estranged siblings often said they wanted from the other sibling. In the case of Rolland and his brother in Chapter 2, a sincere apology from one brother may have led to a reciprocal expression of regret from the other one. They could have repaired their relationship. Rolland could probably have received the apology he longed for. He just may have had to go first.

Often, we find ourselves distanced from someone because we feel they've hurt us. In order to reconnect, we require an apology. But, in a relationship of any length and between entities of any size, everyone involved usually has some grievance with the other. Of course, some injuries are worse than others, warranting serious responsibility for repair, and some occurred first, setting off a cascade of hurt and misunderstanding on both sides. Sometimes, the only route available to restored closeness might require you, like Rolland, first to approach the other with curiosity about *their* experience of hurt and only afterward create a space to address your own.

Much wisdom can be found in the Alcoholics Anonymous (AA) principles and practices. One that particularly catches my interest is the process in AA's Step 4, because it leads you to make amends with people you've hurt. What's startling about this practice is that it begins with listing your resentments, the grudges you've held throughout your life. One by one, you must examine each one of the grudges through a specific lens: With the help of your sponsor, you consider anything you did to contribute to each situation that you resent. In my view, that's a piece of tricky, sophisticated therapy work, one that takes a long time. Ultimately, as I understand it, the idea is that resentments can be transformed into regrets, which you then can take responsibility for. How freeing could that be—to release or, more accurately, transform life-long grudges?

In any case, I'm not recommending that everyone join AA. Nor am I suggesting that you relinquish your feelings of hurt and resentment. I am, however, asking you to consider two ideas: your own possible contributions to your problem situation, and the possible pain the other person carries. It might open up surprising avenues toward resolution.

CHOICES FOR THE HURT PERSON

- Ask for an apology—or not.

- Accept an apology—or not.

- Shape the apology—or not.

- Change the future—or not.

- Forgive—or not.

- Seek vengeance—or not.

- Apologize first—or not.

CHAPTER 10

When *Not* to Apologize

A consistent message throughout *A Good Apology* has been that apologies are valuable and powerful. However, there are times when apologizing is not a good idea.

At fifty-four, Jeremy came to therapy to address a pattern of angry outbursts and related relationship issues with his wife of many years. During the #MeToo movement, he'd also become troubled about an event from long ago, seeing it now in light of male sexual aggression and entitlement. He found himself haunted by guilt about a terrible moment that happened when he was fifteen. After his girlfriend Linda broke up with him, he confronted her at school. When she asked him to leave her alone, he lost his temper and physically restrained her—for a moment—before "coming to his senses" and leaving. Several years ago, she'd reached out to him on social media and they'd developed a friendly "relationship" consisting of occasional messages.

He talked with me about what he wished he could say to Linda

216

now. With a great deal of thought, he drafted and redrafted a letter. All along, he wasn't convinced he would send it, because he was concerned that it might not be in her best interests. What he wrote was a thoughtful and thorough apology. In it, he let her know he was sorry about mistreating her and that he was completely responsible for it. He told her that he had learned important things from his awful mistake and had made sure never to repeat it. He emphasized that he wasn't asking her for anything but would be happy to listen to her if she wanted to talk with him. Finally, at the end of this remarkable letter, he thanked her for her kindness during the entire time they knew each other.

As he worked on the apology letter over several weeks, Jeremy took the opportunity to look at times he'd blown up at his wife in a new, more responsible light. Holding himself accountable for his regrettable behavior many years earlier seemed to enable him to behave better now, too. Perhaps paradoxically, he found himself calmer and less reactive in general than he had felt in years.

As he finished the letter, we discussed his questions around sending it to Linda. He didn't want to remind her of something that had been unpleasant for her at the time and that might no longer even be relevant to her. He realized that the letter hadn't really been written for her well-being, but for his personal resolution. Ultimately, he decided not to send it.

Nonetheless, this apology-that-wasn't helped Jeremy gain self-awareness and make changes for himself and his wife. His decision illustrates the way that practice apology letters can be a good option if the drive to atone is yours alone, and needn't involve the other person.

Sometimes, you may not know for sure how you feel about apologizing to someone. If, for example, you are troubled by a person's painful feelings as a result of your behavior, but you don't regret what you did, you might try to write such a practice letter. Identify all the things you do regret—not that you made the "wrong" choice, but that your actions caused others' pain. The practice apology can help you sort out how you feel and what you might actually want to apologize for.

In addition, there are times when you definitely should not apologize:

WHEN YOU DON'T MEAN IT

If you don't want to hear about someone's reaction to something you've done and you're tempted to say "I'm sorry" to make them stop talking about it, it's likely to backfire. If you are willing to say those two words but not to see through all four steps of the process, it probably won't satisfy anyone. If someone is pressuring you to say the words but you really don't want to, it's better to say something else—or nothing.

WHEN IT WOULD HURT THE OTHER PERSON

In twelve-step programs such as AA, making amends is a major focus of the personal work required. However, AA Step 9 spells out an exception: You must make direct repairs with people you've hurt "wherever possible, *except when to do so would injure them or others.*" (Emphasis mine.)[1] It may be that the harmful experience was too painful, too humiliating, or both, for the other person to want to reopen it. In a recent "The Ethicist" column in the *New York Times Magazine*, Kwame Anthony Appiah concluded, "When an apology from the remote past would simply unearth anguished memories, the right choice may be reticence."[2]

When *Not* to Apologize

I honor this dictum to do no further damage, but I also know it may provide a tempting avoidance excuse. How can you tell the difference between an apology that needs to be made even if it's painful and an apology that you really shouldn't initiate?

WHEN THE PERSON DOESN'T WANT TO HEAR FROM YOU

If the person you hurt has cut off conversation on this subject, then you may not be able to find resolution with them. In an ongoing relationship, the cutoff is often temporary and you'll have another chance to recover together. It's a good idea to leave the conversation open, giving the other person the freedom to decide whether or when the two of you might return to the subject again.

However, if the person you've hurt has asked you not to contact them again, you mustn't. A man asked "The Ethicist" column (a different letter from the one mentioned previously) if he could reach out and apologize to a former friend. He'd gained new insight during the #MeToo movement about how he'd hurt her long ago, but, back then, he'd agreed not to contact her again. In response, Mr. Appiah reminded him that what matters most is what would be good for her now. Although she might value the message that he understood her now, "you aren't entitled to relieve your remaining sense of guilt at her expense."[3]

It's my strong impression that neither the other person's expressed wish that you not contact them, nor your agreement not to, should be violated because you're uncomfortable. It's up to you to deal with your guilt in another forum—say, with a spiritual ritual, a confession to someone else, or vicarious restitution.

WHEN THE PERSON CAN'T RECEIVE IT

What if the person to whom you owe an apology is too young, too unwell, or otherwise too compromised to be able to understand your words and participate with you? Let's say, for example, you were responsible for a tragic car accident that left someone terribly injured. Even though you can't contact the victim or family members, either to apologize or to seek information about the effects of your actions, you may nonetheless feel you owe it to the victim to try to make some kind of repair. Not being able to express your regret directly doesn't rule out conducting a version of the apology steps: Research the effects of the kind of injury you caused or learn about the scope of damage caused by drivers compromised in the way you were. Find a way to share what you've learned or to express your regrets in the form of advocacy. Your sense of responsibility may drive you to seek restitution opportunities, such as contributing to organizations related to your victim's needs. You owe it to both the victim and yourself to do whatever you can to prevent recurrence of the harm, perhaps by teaching others about your mistakes.

When the person with whom you have unfinished amends dies before you can find resolution together, you may carry an extra burden of unresolved feelings. Obviously, you no longer can apologize to the relevant person, but it still behooves you to reconcile with your inner self or with the divine. By some measures, it may actually be more pressing to face your personal regret and responsibility. If you don't, the shadow of the unresolved guilt may color other relationships or your sense of yourself. A "spiritual apology" or confession can involve prayer, ritual, exercises like the letters we've discussed, or a private statement of penitence. It could also involve seeking out a trusted clergyperson or someone else to witness your speaking the truth about your errors. The restitution and prevention opportunities mentioned earlier may also apply.

WHEN A PERSON DEMANDS
TOO MANY APOLOGIES

Let's say you're in a relationship with someone who characteristically overreacts to small things that you don't see as deserving an apology. Early in a relationship, it's often hard to discern whether one person is oversensitive or the other is dismissive of the first one's feelings. This gray area of doubt can be fertile ground for learning to understand one another better, so you both can be kinder—about sensitivities as well as blind spots. And in any given disagreement, that in-between difference in perspective can always arise. A single overreaction from someone you care about always calls for concern and curiosity.

However, advice columnist Carolyn Hax advises that you look at such situations in the aggregate. Over time, you may realize that you are happy to make adjustments out of respect for this person's level of sensitivity, changes that bring you closer. On the other hand, it may become apparent that your partner or your friend is asking you for the impossible, holding you to account for unpredictable disappointments or failures in "mind reading." Their demands for apologies may be unreasonable, and you may decide that it's not right for you to bear the brunt of their complaints.[4]

In response to someone else's pain, empathy is always called for, but self-compassion and personal boundaries are also just as necessary. If you feel yourself to be over a barrel, pressured into apologies you don't understand, or constantly the only one "at fault," it may be better to discontinue repair attempts with that person—at least for a bit. Ask yourself how this pattern came about and what it means to you. Are you involved in a habitual routine that isn't fair or in which you are being controlled or manipulated? If so, can the pattern itself be changed or should you step out of it?

And here, again, there is a crucial distinction to be made between unreasonable pressure from someone else and your own resistance to doing the right thing. Only you can decipher the difference, by listening to your own inner voice and perhaps to a trusted person who is usually reasonable.

Teresa's younger sister Elaine had reminded her of many times from their childhood when Teresa did something that hurt her. Most of the occasions were lost to Teresa's memory because they were very long ago or because they were very minor or both. But, because her sister clearly felt bad about them, Teresa cared. For the most part, she had remained patient and curious, empathic and responsible. Recently, however, Elaine began to demand that Teresa make a particular kind of apology in which she had to describe—sometimes to other family members—details of actions as if she remembered them herself. Elaine maintained that Teresa should trust her, Elaine's, memory about a time Teresa spilled something on her sister's sweater, lied to their parents after a misbehavior, or upstaged her at a family event. Whenever Teresa didn't say things exactly the way Elaine wanted her to, Elaine became furious, left the room, and refused to speak to her for some period of time.

Teresa came in to consult with me because she had a question about apologies. Should she keep making apologies that Elaine seemed to need, even though they had begun to feel wrong to her? We talked about the scenes her sister wanted to create by directing Teresa to say particular lines. Although Elaine's demands for amends had always felt idiosyncratic, Teresa had been willing to give her sister the benefit of the doubt about missing memories. Until now, they hadn't risen to this level of peculiarity and insistence. What was she asking Teresa to enact, and why? Neither of us could tell.

Teresa's task was to find a way to remain kind but not to comply with behavior that felt disturbing to her. Rather than do exactly what Elaine asked, she had to decide what she herself could do honestly and sincerely. As she realized, that meant she had to stop apologizing for things she didn't remember. At the same time, she wanted to help soothe her sister's pain. She brainstormed ways to support Elaine while maintaining her boundaries.

If you're caught up in any relationship that doesn't operate on healthy, reciprocal patterns, what should you do about apologizing? What if the other person not only would fail to make good use of your apology, but would even misuse it? Experience may teach you that your willingness to be humble and vulnerable in an openhearted apology is not psychologically safe with this person. If that turns out to be the case, your task becomes protecting yourself. You have to establish your limits and hold to them, not allowing yourself to be drawn into harmful interactions. If the other person doesn't honor your boundaries—say, won't discontinue a coercive conversation that you need to postpone or interrupt—you may need to leave the physical space. In such relationships, the question becomes whether or not you can work together enough to make the major changes needed, bigger ones than an apology from you can fix.

WHEN YOUR APOLOGY IS NEVER-ENDING

To heal from a relationship injury can take a long time. What counts as too long? You may have witnessed a relationship that's stuck in unbalanced roles. This can, for example, show up where one person seems always to be seeking forgiveness or acceptability, as if they are permanently a second-class citizen, having to prove their right to be there; whereas the other person has become accustomed to adopting a preemptive moral advantage in any dispute, or their woundedness be- comes a habitual rebuke. These patterns indicate that an apology has gone awry or become rigidly frozen partway through. It's in no one's best interests to be perpetually the victim, nor is it good for you to feel like you're in the doghouse forever.

You can shift this corrupted pattern, this stuck-in-midstream, incomplete apology. It may help you to consider the possibility of redemption. What would it look like in your case? How can you identify what's needed to make things right? In your ideal, wished-for outcome, what do you want this relationship to become? Can you both remember the idea of compassionate accountability for mistakes, even major missteps? Can you step outside your familiar patterns enough to find a shared "mountain moment" like the one Jonny and Sarah found, when they clarified their values? What would shift the frame of your history enough to allow a different future? What could allow both members of the couple to have a fresh view of their relationship? If you can't find your way to unstick this corrupted pattern on your own, you might want to try couples therapy. Often, a stubborn pattern can benefit from the perspective of a trusted third party.

The liveliness of a healthy relationship that has healed from problems they've faced together feels very different from this kind of stuckness. Couples who've successfully survived infidelity may have to revisit the issue periodically, but they don't stay there.

WHEN YOU NEVER DO ANYTHING WRONG

Okay, this one is almost a joke, but some people actually do believe that they are never at fault. They think that if you only minded your step and lived with conviction, like they do, you wouldn't make mistakes, either.

I don't believe in original sin (a Roman Catholic doctrine), but I know it's almost impossible to avoid participating in some exploitative venture, even if it's by buying chocolate that's linked to abusive child labor practices, or investing in mutual funds that somehow support diamond mines or drive local enterprises out of business. Although we can take steps to minimize these connections, in our current, complex culture, there is "blood" on almost everyone's hands. I would argue that the moral solution here is not necessarily to apologize more, but to live as deliberately as you can, leave as little damage behind you as you can, and try to heal the damage you do cause.

WHEN IT'S BETTER *NOT* TO APOLOGIZE

- When it's only for your benefit

- When you don't mean it

- When it would hurt the other person

- When the person doesn't want to hear from you

- When the person can't receive it

- When a person demands too many apologies

- When your apology is never-ending

- When you haven't done anything wrong

CONCLUSION

You Can Make Things Right

Thank you for spending this time with me. Together we've walked through stories of people struggling and stumbling and mostly finding their ways to greater integrity and more loving connections. I hope you've thought about your own relationships and the apologies that might heal breaches for you. I hope you remember the change in mind-set that allows you to listen deeply to someone whose perspective is different from yours.

The lessons in this book are old-fashioned and timeless: Listen with an open mind, take responsibility for your actions, speak with empathy, and make things right with other people. As such, they are potential targets for mockery, particularly in a postmodern age that de-values sincerity and prizes ironic detachment. I've no defense against the claim of uncoolness. I'm going for something deeper—because there is nothing like an apology, nothing so vast in its impact and yet so personal in its execution, so powerful and so small.

Like others before me, I've probably written the book I needed to read.

As I worked on *A Good Apology,* I sorted through the hundreds of newspaper clippings and online articles I've printed out. Only a relative handful made their way into the book, but I've reread them all. I appreciate the stories of those who've made valiant attempts to apologize. I admire those who've demanded the apologies they deserved. I celebrate the "happy endings" we can all feel, the satisfying resolutions, the healing.

I'm not a particularly harmful person, nor have I led a painless, charmed life. Nonetheless, at this relatively seasoned stage of life, my own regrets seem to outnumber my grudges. Moreover, since I've been working on this project, I'm at times even plagued by hurts I don't know about—you know, because of how poorly we detect our own missteps.

After the years I've spent on this topic, what I'm left with is a tender call to arms—by which I don't mean weapons, but I do mean fierceness. My personal commitment to live the way I've described in this book is daunting, but seems crucially important.

I imagine a world where we all seek common ground and common purpose more than we seek dominance and being right. I imagine taking the heavy stones of shame and resentment from our pockets and stepping more lightly toward one another. I imagine holding myself and my loved ones accountable in a more compassionate way.

Writing this book has helped me open my heart more toward the people who've hurt me and become less defensive toward those giving me feedback I don't like hearing. If you are someone I've hurt, please let me know that, and let me try to make it right.

Wherever the ideas in this book take you, dear reader, may you be accompanied by courage and compassion. Be in touch. Let me know how it works out.

WHAT IF?

What if there's a way to promote healing for someone else, improve your health, enhance your spiritual life, enrich your relationships, and contribute to a more trusting community? What if this powerful way is free and available to everyone, regardless of special skills or resources? What if you know how to do this magical thing? Is there any reason weighty enough to keep you from doing it?

Acknowledgments

I've been noodling around the topic of apologies for decades. I am grateful for the intellectual, spiritual, and artistic communities that have supported my long search for ways to tell these stories. This particular book has come about as a direct result of the belief Leah Miller, editor at Grand Central Publishing, had in its value, long before I did. A deep bow and a thank-you to you, Leah. I'd also like to express my appreciation for Katherine Flynn of Kneerim & Williams, for being the kindest, smartest, and most supportive agent I can imagine. To Haley Weaver, Carolyn Kurek, Eileen Chetti, Alana Spendley, and others at GCP whose names I don't know, thank you for making this manuscript into an honest-to-goodness book I can hold in my hand.

To the Grub Street writing center, and instructors Michele Seaton, Ethan Gilsdorf, Pagan Kennedy, Alex Marzano-Lesnevich, Ogi Ogas, Steve Almond, and Matthew Fredrick, I am forever in your debt for teaching me to be a writer. For the psychology departments at Florida State University and Beth Israel Hospital, for teaching me how to be a psychologist, and especially to Drs. Jack Hokanson and Marian Winterbottom, for showing me how to be a decent person, I will always be grateful. For their many hours of listening and caring, thank you to Drs. Bernard Levine and Alexandra Harrison.

To editor extraordinaire and my oldest friend, Rebecca Wilson, thank you for both your gritty grammatical knowledge and our neverending conversation about things that matter. To those trusted friends

Acknowledgments

and colleagues who read draft after draft, always with fresh eyes and willingness to critique, I appreciate you more than you may ever know: Donna Luff, Barbara Williamson, Jan Love, Ellen Golding, Carol Gray, and the remarkable women of the Hive (Carroll Sandel, Meg Senuta, Ann MacDonald, Shelby Meyerhoff, and Judy Bolton-Fasman).

For her knowledge of psychological thought, particular appreciation goes to Dr. Ellen Golding; for her work in health care communications, to Dr. Donna Luff; for his neuroscience expertise, to Dr. Per Sederberg; for their understanding of spiritual matters, to the Reverends Barbara Williamson and Nathan Detering and Dr. Jan Love; for introducing me to concepts in transformative justice, to Jessica James; and for their insights about management and organizations, to Janna Bubley, Matt Bubley, and Jesse Buckingham.

For their undying faith in me, their deep comfort in dark times, and their celebration of my successes, I will always be grateful to my Dream Circle (Joy, Denise, Vera, Pam, Carol, Gianna, and Deed) and the Farm Pond Sisters (Kit, Susie, Mary, Sue, and Kim). For the beloved community that keeps me working toward a more just and balanced world, I am indebted to the people of the Unitarian Universalist Area Church in Sherborn, Massachusetts—including the Swarm. Thank you to many others for your kindness and for engaging in conflict that didn't destroy our relationships.

And my families! To the people I come from (my ancestors, my parents, Bob, Bill and Elsie, Byron, my amazing nieces and nephews, and Glenn), thank you for all the ways you've helped me grow and become who I am. To the family I'm blessed to call my own now (Matt, Janna, Eliza, and Jackson), thank you all for your astonishing gifts and your depth, your connection and your challenge, and your love and support. And to my beloved, Peter, I am forever full of gratitude for your presence in my life, for standing by me with tenderness and humor, and for the enormous favor of seeing my ideas as valid when I'm afraid to trust them myself.

Notes

INTRODUCTION

1   Teddy Wayne, "Choose Your Own Public Apology," *New York Times*, November 24, 2017.

2   Lynn Martire and Melissa Franks, eds., "The Role of Social Networks in Adult Health," special issue, *Health Psychology* 53, no. 6 (2014).

3   Timothy Smith and Anne Kazak, eds., "Close Family Relationships and Health," special issue, *American Psychologist* 72, no. 6 (2017).

4   Jason Daley, "The UK Now Has a 'Minister for Loneliness.' Here's Why It Matters," Smithsonian.com, January 19, 2018.

5   Gretchen Anderson, *Loneliness Among Older Adults: A National Survey of Adults 45+* (Washington, DC: AARP, 2010).

6   Vivek Murthy, "Work and the Loneliness Epidemic: Reducing Isolation at Work Is Good for Business," *Harvard Business Review*, September 2017.

7   Carol Gilligan, *In a Different Voice: Psychological Theory and Women's Development* (Cambridge, MA: Harvard University Press, 1982).

8   Heinz Kohut, *The Restoration of the Self* (New York: International Universities Press, 1977).

9   Jean Baker Miller, *Toward a New Psychology of Women* (Boston: Beacon Press, 1976).

CHAPTER 1. WHY APOLOGIZE?

1   Kelsey Borresen, "11 Things the Happiest Couples Say to Each Other All the Time," *HuffPost*, February 7, 2019, Relationships.

2   Daphne de Marneffe, "The Secret to a Happy Marriage Is Knowing How to Fight," *New York Times*, January 12, 2018.

3   Geoffrey Bromiley, *Theological Dictionary of the New Testament*, abridged in 1 vol. (Grand Rapids, MI: William B. Eerdmans, 1985).

4   Gordon Marino, "What's the Use of Regret?" *New York Times*, November 12, 2016.

5   Avi Klein, "A Psychotherapist's Plea to Louis C.K.," *New York Times*, January 6, 2019.

6   Anne Lamott, *Help, Thanks, Wow: The Three Essential Prayers* (New York: Riverhead Books, 2012).

7   Alicia Wittmeyer, "Eight Stories of Men's Regret," *New York Times*, October 18, 2018.

8   Nick Ferraro, "30 Years Later, Minn. Hit-and-Run Driver Sends $1,000 to Police to Give to Victim," *St. Paul Pioneer Press*, November 29, 2017.

9   Julianne Holt-Lunstadt, Timothy Smith, and J. Bradley Layton, "Social Relationships and Mortality Risk: A Meta-Analytical Review," *PLOS Medicine* 7 (2010), https://doi.org/10.1371/journalpmed.1000316.

10   Lynn Martire and Melissa Franks, eds., "The Role of Social Networks in Adult Health," special issue, *Health Psychology* 53, no. 6 (2014); Timothy Smith and Anne Kazak, eds., "Close Family Re-

lationships and Health," special issue, *American Psychologist* 72, no. 6 (2017).

11   Vivek Murthy, "Work and the Loneliness Epidemic: Reducing Isolation at Work Is Good for Business," *Harvard Business Review*, September 2017.

12   Max Fisher, "Yes, Netanyahu's Apology to Turkey Is a Very Big Deal," *Washington Post*, March 22, 2013.

13   Senator Sam Brownback, "A Joint Resolution to Acknowledge a Long History of Official Depredations and Ill-Conceived Policies by the Federal Government Regarding Indian Tribes and Offer an Apology to All Native Peoples on Behalf of the United States," S.J. Res. 14, 111th Cong. (April 30, 2009), https://www.congress.gov /bill/111th-congress/senate-joint-resolution/14.

14   Rob Capriccioso, "A Sorry Saga: Obama Signs Native American Apology Resolution, Fails to Draw Attention to It," *Indian Country Today*, January 13, 2010.

15   Layli Long Soldier, *Whereas* (Minneapolis, MN: Greywolf, 2017).

16   John Kador, *Effective Apology: Mending Fences, Building Bridges, and Restoring Trust* (San Francisco: Berrett-Koehler, 2009), 7.

17   Kador, 15.

18   Kador, 3.

19   Leigh Anthony, "Why Do Businesses Need Customer Complaints?" *Small Business—Chron.com*, accessed July 13, 2019, https://smallbusiness.chron.com/businesses-need-customer -complaints-2042.html#.

20   Daniella Kupor, Taly Reich, and Kristin Laurin, "The (Bounded) Benefits of Correction: The Unanticipated Interpersonal Advantages of Making and Correcting Mistakes," *Organizational Behavior and Human Decision Processes* 149 (November 2018), https://doi.org/10.1016/j.obhdp.2018.08.002.

21   Patrick Lencioni, *The Five Dysfunctions of a Team Summarized for Busy People* (Bloomington, IN: Partridge Publishers, 2017).

Notes

22 Lisa Earle McLeod, "Why Avoiding Conflict Keeps You Trapped in It Forever," *HuffPost*, July 6, 2011.

23 Amy Edmondson, "Psychological Safety and Learning Behavior in Work Teams," *Administrative Science Quarterly* 44, no. 2 (1999).

24 Amy Edmondson, "Creating Psychological Safety in the Workplace," *Harvard Business Review Ideacast*, January 22, 2019.

25 James Baldwin, "As Much Truth as One Can Bear: To Speak Out About the World as It Is, Says James Baldwin, Is the Writer's Job," *New York Times Book Review*, January 14, 1962.

26 Judith Glaser, "Your Brain Is Hooked on Being Right," *Harvard Business Review*, February 2, 2013.

27 Bert Uchino and Baldwin Way, "Integrative Pathways Linking Close Family Ties to Health: A Neurochemical Perspective," *American Psychologist* 72, no. 6 (September 2017).

28 Tom Delbanco and Sigall Bell, "Guilty, Afraid and Alone—Struggling with Medical Error," *New England Journal of Medicine* 357 (2007).

29 Darshak Sanghavi, "Medical Malpractice"

30 Delbanco and Bell, "Guilty."

31 Allen Kachalia et al., "Liability Claims and Costs Before and After Implementation of a Medical Error Disclosure Program," *Annals of Internal Medicine* 153 (2010).

32 Sanghavi, "Medical Malpractice: Why Is It So Hard for Doctors to Apologize?" *Boston Globe*, January 27, 2013.

33 Editorial Staff, "With Respectful Apology, Boston Police Defuse Tensions," *Boston Globe*, May 6, 2015.

34 Yawu Miller, "Boston Sees Profound Political Changes in 2018," *Bay State Banner*, December 28, 2018.

35 Steve Brown, "7 Key Provisions of the Criminal Justice Bill," *WBUR News*, April 6, 2018, https://www.wbur.org/news/2018/04/06/criminal-justice-reform-bill-key-provisions.

36   Eric Pfeiffer, "SNL Star Pete Davidson's Apology to This War Veteran Turned into a Moving Call for Unity," Upworthy, November 12, 2018, https://www.upworthy.com/snl-star-pete -davidson-s-apology-to-this-war-veteran-turned-into-a-moving -call-for-unity.

CHAPTER 2. IT'S SO VERY HARD TO DO

1   Sara Eckel, "Why Siblings Sever Ties," *Psychology Today* (March 9, 2015).

2   Lucy Blake, Becca Bland, and Susan Golombok, "Hidden Voices—Family Estrangement in Adulthood," University of Cambridge (December 10, 2015), http://standalone.org.uk/wp -content/uploads/2015/12/HiddenVoices.-Press.pdf.

3   Kathryn Schulz, *Being Wrong: Adventures in the Margin of Error* (New York: HarperCollins, 2010).

4   Schulz, 4.

5   Judith Glaser, "Your Brain Is Hooked on Being Right," *Harvard Business Review*, February 2, 2013.

6   Evan Andrews, "Seven Bizarre Witch Trial Tests," History.com, March 18, 2013, https://www.history.com/news/7-bizarre-witch -trial-tests.

7   Christopher Chabris and Daniel Simons, *The Invisible Gorilla: How Our Intuitions Deceive Us* (New York: Random House, 2010).

8   Daniel Simons, "The Monkey Business Illusion," theinvisible gorilla.com, April 28, 2010, https://www.youtube.com/watch ?v=IGQmdoK_ZfY.

9   Trafton Drew, Melissa Vo, and Jeremy Wolfe, "The Invisible Go-rilla Strikes Again: Sustained Inattentional Blindness in Expert Observers," *Psychological Science* 24, no. 9 (2013).

10 Leon Festinger, Henry Riecken, and Stanley Schachter, *When Prophecy Fails: A Social and Psychological Study of a Modern Group That Predicted the Destruction of the World* (Minneapolis: University of Minnesota Press, 1956).

11 D. Westen et al., "The Neural Basis of Motivated Reasoning: An fMRI Study of Emotional Constraints on Political Judgment During the US Presidential Election of 2004," *Journal of Cognitive Neuroscience* 18 (2006).

12 Carol Tavris and Elliot Aronson, *Mistakes Were Made (But Not by Me): Why We Justify Foolish Beliefs, Bad Decisions, and Hurtful Acts* (San Diego, CA: Harcourt, 2007).

13 Stephanie Pappas, "APA Issues First-Ever Guidelines for Practice with Men and Boys," *American Psychological Association Monitor* 50 (2019).

14 Nile Gardiner and Morgan Roach, "Barack Obama's Top 10 Apologies: How the President Has Humiliated a Superpower," Heritage Foundation, June 2, 2009, https://www.heritage.org/europe/report/barack-obamas-top-10-apologies-how-the-president-has-humiliated-superpower.

15 Mitt Romney, *No Apology: The Case for American Greatness* (New York: St. Martin's Press, 2010).

16 Blake, Bland, and Golombok, "Hidden Voices."

17 Rosalind Wiseman, *Masterminds and Wingmen: Helping Our Boys Cope with Schoolyard Power, Locker-Room Tests, Girlfriends, and the New Rules of Boy World* (New York: Harmony Books, 2013).

18 Patrick Lencioni, *The Five Dysfunctions of a Team Summarized for Busy People* (Bloomington, IN: Partridge Publishers, 2017).

19 David Larcker et al., "2013 Executive Coaching Survey," Stanford University Graduate School of Business and the Miles Group, August 2013, https://www.gsb.stanford.edu/faculty-research/publications/2013-executive-coaching-survey.

20 Nicolette Amarillas, "It's Time for Women to Stop Apologizing So Much," *WOMEN/Entrepreneur*, July 12, 2018, https://www.entrepreneur.com/article/314199.

21   Kristin Wong, "Negotiating While Female: How to Talk About Your Salary," *New York Times*, June 16, 2019, Working Woman's Handbook Issue.

22   Ian Ferguson and Will Ferguson, *How to Be a Canadian (Even If You Already Are One)* (Vancouver: Douglas & McIntyre, 2007).

23   Jacey Fortin, "After an 'Ambiguous' Apology for Ryan Adams, What's the Right Way to Say Sorry?" *New York Times*, February 15, 2019.

CHAPTER 3. IT'S NOT EASY, BUT IT'S NOT MYSTERIOUS

1   "The Ash Wednesday Liturgy," *Book of Common Prayer* (New York: Church Publishing, 1979).

2   Peter Beaulieu, *Beyond Secularism and Jihad? A Triangular Inquiry into the Mosque, the Manger, and Modernity* (Lanham, MD: University Press of America, 2012).

3   K. C. Lee et al., "Repentance in Chinese Buddhism: Implications for Mental Health Professionals," *Journal of Spirituality in Mental Health* 19, no. 3 (2017); published online July 13, 2016.

4   Hsing Yun, "Repentance," *Being Good*, accessed on Fo Guang Shan International Translation Center website, May 28, 2018, https://www.fgsitc.org.

5   Patrick Lencioni, *The Five Dysfunctions of a Team Summarized for Busy People* (Bloomington, IN: Partridge Publishers, 2017).

6   Kim Scott, *Radical Candor: How to Get What You Want by Saying What You Mean* (New York: St. Martin's Press, 2019).

7   *Alcoholics Anonymous (The Big Book)*, 4th ed. (New York: Alcoholics Anonymous World Service, 2001).

8   Martine Powers, "On Yom Kippur, Atonement via Twitter," *Boston Globe*, September 22, 2012.

9   Postsecret.com website; "PostSecret: Private Secrets Shared Anonymously with the World," *CBS News*, April 28, 2019, https://www.cbsnews.com/news/postsecret-private-secrets-anonymously-shared-with-the-world/.

10 Pope Benedict XVI, "Pope Benedict's Final Homily," Salt and Light Media, February 8, 2018, https://saltandlighttv.org/blogfeed/getpost.php?id=44496.

11 Stephen Mitchell, "Attachment Theory and the Psychoanalytic Tradition: Reflections of Human Relationality," *Psychoanalytic Dialogues* 9, no. 1 (1999).

12 Juana Bordas, *Salsa, Soul, and Spirit: Leadership for a Multicultural Age*, 2nd ed. (San Francisco: Berrett-Koehler, 2012).

13 Michael Meade, "The Wise and the Crosswise," Living Myth, podcast 105, https://www.livingmyth.org/living-myth-podcast-105-the-wise-and-the-crosswise.

14 Robert E. Maydole, "Aquinas' Third Way Modalized," in *Proceedings of the Twentieth World Congress of Philosophy*, ed. Jaakko Hintikka et al. (Boston: August 1998), https://www.bu.edu/wcp/Papers/Reli/ReliMayd.htm.

15 Niall Dickson, "UK Politics: What Is the Third Way?" *BBC News*, September 27, 1999.

16 Henry Kamm, "For Peres, Pullout Has Moral Value," *New York Times*, May 1, 1985.

17 Emily Sweeney, "US Attorney Says Loughlin Could Face a 'Higher Sentence,'" *Boston Globe*, October 9, 2019.

18 Centre for Justice and Reconciliation: A Program of Prison Fellowship International website, http://restorativejustice.org/#sthash.YajhsOhY.dpbs.

19 Howard Zehr, *The Little Book of Restorative Justice*, rev. and updated (New York: Skyhorse Publishing, 2015).

20 Sandra Pavelka, "Restorative Justice in the States: An Analysis of Statutory Legislation and Policy," *Justice Policy Journal* 2 (Fall 2016).

21   Michelle Alexander, "Reckoning with Violence," *New York Times*, March 3, 2019, citing Danielle Sered's *Until We Reckon*.

22   Richard Boothman, "Fifteen + One: What (I Think) I've Learned," address at MACRMI (Massachusetts Alliance for Communication and Resolution Following Medical Injury) CARe Forum, Waltham, MA, May 7, 2019.

23   Thomas Gallagher and Amy Waterman, "Patients' and Physicians' Attitudes Regarding the Disclosure of Medical Errors," *Journal of the American Medical Association* 289, no. 8 (2003).

24   Jennifer Moore, Kathleen Bismark, and Michelle Mello, "Patients' Experiences with Communication-and-Resolution Programs after Medical Injury," *JAMA Internal Medicine* 177, no. 11 (2017).

25   John Kador, *Effective Apology: Mending Fences, Building Bridges, and Restoring Trust* (San Francisco: Berrett-Koehler Publishers, 2009).

26   Kim LaCapria, "Jason Alexander's Apology for Gay Joke Is Like Basically a Primer on Both Apologies and Being Nice to Gay People," *Inquisitr*, June 5, 2012, https://www.inquisitr.com/247977/jason-alexanders-apology-for-gay-joke-is-like-basically-a-primer-on-both-apologies-and-being-nice-to-gay-people/.

27   Greg Rienzi, "Other Nations Could Learn from Germany's Efforts to Reconcile After WWII," *Johns Hopkins Magazine*, Summer 2015.

28   Lily Gardner Feldman, "Reconciliation Means Having to Say You're Sorry," *Foreign Policy*, April 2, 2014.

29   Bilal Qureshi, "From Wrong to Right: A US Apology for Japanese Internment," National Public Radio, August 9, 2013.

30   Civil Liberties Act of 1988, Densho Encyclopedia website: http://encyclopedia.densho.org/Civil_Liberties_Public_Education_Fund/.

31   Bob Egelko, "California Expands Japanese Internment Education to Current Rights Threats," *San Francisco Chronicle*, September 30, 2017.

32   Claire Zillman, "'I Am Sorry. We Are Sorry.' Read Justin

Trudeau's Formal Apology to Canada's LGBTQ Community," *Fortune*, November 29, 2017, https://fortune.com/2017/11/29 /justin-trudeau-lgbt-apology-full-transcript/.

33 Joanna Smith, "'I Am Sorry. We Are Sorry': Trudeau Apologizes on Behalf of Canada for Past Discrimination," *Toronto Sun*, November 28, 2018.

34 Gary Nguyen, "Canada Apologizes for Denying Asylum to Jewish Refugees of the MS St. Louis in 1939," *World Religion News*, November 12, 2018.

35 Catherine Porter, "Trudeau Apologizes for Canada's Turning Away Ship of Jews Fleeing Nazis," *New York Times*, November 7, 2018.

36 June Tangney, "Two Faces of Shame: The Roles of Shame and Guilt in Predicting Recidivism," *Psychological Science* (March 2014).

37 Joseph Goldstein, "An Afternoon with Joseph Goldstein," Dharma Seed website, April 25, 2005, https://dharmaseed.org /teacher/96/talk/42970/.

38 Brené Brown, "Listening to Shame," TED2012, Long Beach, CA, March 2012, https://www.ted.com/talks/brene_brown_listening _to_shame?language=en.

CHAPTER 4. STEP ONE: DON'T JUST DO SOMETHING; STAND THERE

1 Tal Eyal, Mary Steffel, and Nicholas Epley, "Perspective Mistaking: Accurately Understanding the Mind of Another Requires Getting Perspective, Not Taking Perspective," *Journal of Personality and Social Psychology* 111, no. 4 (2018).

2 Leslie Jamison, *The Empathy Exams* (Minneapolis, MN: Greywolf Press, 2014).

Notes

3   Peter Wehner, "Seeing Trump Through a Glass, Darkly," *New York Times*, October 7, 2017.

4   Tom Coens and Mary Jenkins, "Why People Don't Get Feedback at Work," in *Abolishing Performance Appraisals: Why They Backfire and What to Do Instead* (San Francisco: Berrett-Koehler, 2000).

5   Gideon Nave et al., "Single Dose Testosterone Administration Impairs Cognitive Reflection in Men," *Psychological Science* 28, no. 10 (August 3, 2017).

6   "What Is Self Psychology?—An Introduction," Self Psychology Psychoanalysis website, http://www.selfpsychologypsychoanalysis .org/whatis.shtml.

7   Harville Hendrix, *Getting the Love You Want: A Guide for Couples* (New York: Henry Holt, 1998).

8   Martha Minow, *Between Vengeance and Forgiveness: Facing History After Genocide and Mass Violence* (Boston: Beacon Press, 1998).

9   Minow, 71.

10 Janice Love, *Southern Africa in World Politics: Local Aspirations and Global Entanglements* (Boulder, CO: Westview Press, 2005).

11 Richard Boothman, "Fifteen + One: What (I Think) I've Learned," address at MACRMI (Massachusetts Alliance for Communication and Resolution Following Medical Injury) CARe Forum, Waltham, MA, May 7, 2019.

12 Cris Beam, "I Did a Terrible Thing. How Can I Apologize?" *New York Times*, June 30, 2018.

13 Brené Brown, *Dare to Lead: Brave Work. Tough Conversations. Whole Hearts.* (New York: Random House, 2018).

14 Brené Brown, *Daring Greatly: How the Courage to Be Vulnerable Transforms the Way We Live, Love, Parent and Lead* (New York: Penguin Random House, 2012).

15 Thomas Curran and Andrew Hill, "Perfectionism Is Increasing over Time: A Meta-Analysis of Birth Cohort Differences from 1989 to 2016," *Psychological Bulletin* 145, no. 4 (2019).

16   Kenneth Jones and Tema Okun, "The Characteristics of White Supremacy Culture," *Dismantling Racism: A Workbook for Social Change Groups*, ChangeWork, 2001, http://www.dismantling racism.org.

17   Winston Churchill, "Monday Motivation: Words of Wisdom to Get Your Week Started," *Telegraph*, October 10, 2016.

18   Kim Scott, *Radical Candor: How to Get What You Want by Saying What You Mean* (New York: St. Martin's Press, 2019).

19   Janelle Nanos, "The Negative Feedback Trap," *Boston Globe Magazine*, October 28, 2018.

20   Adrienne Maree Brown, "What Is/Isn't Transformative Justice?" *Adrienne Maree Brown* blog, July 9, 2015, http://adriennemareebrown.net /2015/07/09/what-isisnt-transformative-justice/.

21   Galway Kinnell, "Crying," *Mortal Acts and Mortal Words* (Boston: Houghton Mifflin, 1980).

22   Lisa Earle McLeod, "Why Avoiding Conflict Prolongs It," McLeod and More website, January 22, 2019, https://www.mcleodandmore .com/2019/01/22/why-avoiding-conflict-prolongs-it/.

23   "Victim Offender Panels," Centre for Justice and Reconciliation. http://restorativejustice.org/restorative-justice/about -restorative-justice/tutorial-intro-to-restorative-justice/lesson-3 -programs/victim-offender-panels/#sthash.aynryHl2.dpbs.

CHAPTER 5. STEP TWO: SAY IT AND MEAN IT

1   Avi Klein, "A Psychotherapist's Plea to Louis C.K.," *New York Times*, January 6, 2019.

2   Marcia Ingall, "Zuckerberg and the Terrible, Horrible, No-Good, Very Bad Apologies," *SorryWatch* blog, April 11, 2018, http://www.sorrywatch.com/?s=zuckerberg.

Notes

3   Daniel Ames and Susan Fiske, "Intent to Harm: Willful Acts Seem More Damaging," *Psychological Science* (2013).

4   Pema Chodron, "The Answer to Anger and Aggression Is Patience," Lion's Roar: Buddhist Wisdom for Our Time website, March 1, 2005, https://www.lionsroar.com.

5   Kathryn Schulz, *Being Wrong: Adventures in the Margin of Error* (New York: HarperCollins, 2010).

6   Judith Glaser, "Your Brain Is Hooked on Being Right," *Harvard Business Review*, February 2, 2013.

7   Patricia Love and Steven Stosny, *How to Improve Your Marriage Without Talking About It* (New York: Broadway Books, 2007).

8   Darshak Sanghavi, "Medical Malpractice: Why Is It So Hard for Doctors to Apologize?" *Boston Globe*, January 27, 2013.

9   *Guardian* staff and agencies, "Biden Condemns 'White Man's Culture' as He Laments Role in Anita Hill Hearings," *Guardian*, March 26, 2019.

10 Matt Stevens, "Biden Declines to Apologize for Role in Thomas Hearing," *Boston Globe*, April 27, 2019.

11 Moira Donegan, "Anita Hill Deserves a Real Apology. Why Couldn't Joe Biden Offer One?" *Guardian*, April 26, 2019.

12 Robert Truog et al., *Talking with Patients and Families About Medical Error: A Guide for Education and Practice* (Baltimore, MD: Johns Hopkins University Press, 2011).

13 Carol Tavris and Elliot Aronson, *Mistakes Were Made (But Not by Me): Why We Justify Foolish Beliefs, Bad Decisions, and Hurtful Acts* (San Diego, CA: Harcourt, 2007).

14 Jack Bauer and Heidi Wayment, "The Psychology of the Quiet Ego," in *Decade of Behavior. Transcending Self-Interest: Psychological Explorations of the Quiet Ego*, ed. Heidi Wayment and Jack Bauer (Washington, DC: American Psychological Association, 2008).

15 Ruth Whippman, "Why 'Lean In'? It's Time for Men to 'Lean Out,'" *New York Times*, October 13, 2019.

16 Jim Collins, "Level 5 Leadership: The Triumph of Humility and Fierce Resolve," *Harvard Business Review*, July–August 2005.

17 Truog et al., *Talking with Patients*.

18 Former CEO of BIDMC Paul Levy, personal communication, April 23, 2019.

19 Michael Barbaro, host, "A High School Assault," *The Daily* podcast, September 20, 2018, https://www.nytimes.com/2018/09/20/podcasts/the-daily/kavanaugh-christine-blasey-ford-caitlin-flanagan-sexual-assault.html.

20 Lindsey Weber, "Celebrities Tap Their Apologies," *New York Times*, January 13, 2019.

21 Meghan Irons, "At Panel on Racial Terms, a Line Is Crossed," *Boston Globe*, February 8, 2019.

22 *Globe* Editorial Staff, "After UN Apology, Real Work in Haiti Begins," *Boston Globe*, December 5, 2016.

23 Adrian Walker, "UN Apology Hard-Earned," *Boston Globe*, December 5, 2016.

24 Donna Moriarty, "Stop Apologizing and Say These Things Instead," *Fast Company*, April 14, 2019.

25 Amy Dickinson, "Woman Regrets Inaction over Campus Abuse Allegation," *Boston Globe*, October 8, 2018.

26 Molly Howes, "The Power of a Good Apology," WBUR *Cognoscenti* blog, October 11, 2018, https://www.wbur.org/cognoscenti/2018/10/11/me-too-how-to-apologize-molly-howes.

27 Alicia Wittmeyer, "Eight Stories of Men's Regret," *New York Times*, October 18, 2018.

28 Nancy Updike, "Get a Spine," *This American Life*, May 10, 2019, https://www.thisamericanlife.org/674/transcript.

29 Peter DeMarco, "Losing Laura," *Boston Globe Magazine*, November 3, 2018.

30 Priyanka Dayal McClusky, "Hospital Leaders Apologize, Ac-

knowledge Mistakes That Cost Laura Levis Her Life," *Boston Globe*, November 13, 2018.

CHAPTER 6. STEP THREE: DEBTS, IOUS, AND MAKING THINGS WHOLE

1   Brandi Miller, "White People Owe Us an Apology, but We Don't Owe Them Forgiveness," *HuffPost* (October 21, 2018).

2   Alice Liu, "Every Moment a Touchpoint for Building Trust," Wharton Work/Life Integration Project, May 14, 2014, http://worklife.wharton.upenn.edu/2014/05/every-moment-touchpoint-building-trust-doug-conant/.

3   Carolyn Hax, "Readers Discuss Recoupling Special Days," *Washington Post*, July 2018.

4   Jared Marcelle, "Meatball and Chain," *This American Life*, February 15, 2019, https://www.thisamericanlife.org/668/the-long-fuse/act-three-5.

5   Frank Scheck, "'A Better Man': Film Review," *Hollywood Reporter*, May 8, 2017.

6   Arwa Mahdai, "Attiya Khan: Why I Confronted the Boyfriend Who Beat Me—and Made a Film About It," *Guardian*, November 15, 2017.

7   Doreen St. Felix, "After Abuse, the Possibility of 'A Better Man,'" *New Yorker*, November 19, 2017.

8   Gary Chapman and Jennifer Thomas, *When Sorry Isn't Enough* (Chicago: Northfield Publishing, 2013).

9   James McAuley, "France Admits to Torture During Algerian War," *Boston Globe*, September 13, 2018.

10 Rachel Swarms, "Georgetown University Plans Steps to Atone for Slave Past," *New York Times*, September 1, 2016.

Notes

11 Susan Svrluga, "'Make It Right': Descendants of Slaves Demand Restitution from Georgetown," *Washington Post*, January 17, 2018.

12 Tressie McMillan Cottom, "Georgetown's Slavery Announcement Is Remarkable. But It's Not Reparations," *Vox*, September 2, 2016, https://www.vox.com/2016/9/2/12773110/georgetown-slavery -admission-reparations.

13 Martin Pengelly, "Georgetown Students Vote to Pay Reparations for Slaves Sold by University," *Guardian*, April 15, 2019.

14 Juliet Isselbacher and Molly McCafferty, "Agassiz's Descendants Urge Harvard to Turn Over Slave Photos," *Harvard Crimson*, June 21, 2019.

15 Jill Filipovic, "Let Us Now Punish Famous Men," *Time*, May 21, 2018.

16 Jonathan Shay, *Achilles in Vietnam: Combat Trauma and the Undoing of Character* (New York: Scribner, 1995).

17 Aaron Pratt Shepherd, "For Veterans, a Path to Healing 'Moral Injury,'" *New York Times*, December 9, 2017.

18 Robert Meagher and Douglas Pryer, eds., *War and Moral Injury: A Reader* (Eugene, OR: Cascade Books, 2018).

19 David Brooks, "The Case for Reparations: A Slow Convert to the Cause," *New York Times*, March 7, 2019.

20 Katrina Browne, *Traces of the Trade: A Story from the Deep North*, https://vimeo.com/ondemand/tracesofthetradea.

21 Ta-Nehisi Coates, "The Case for Reparations," *Atlantic*, June 2014.

22 Brooks, "The Case."

23 Patricia Cohen, "What Reparations for Slavery Might Look Like in 2019," *New York Times*, May 23, 2019.

24 Michael Eric Dyson, *Tears We Cannot Stop: A Sermon to White America* (New York: St. Martin's Press, 2017).

Notes

CHAPTER 7. STEP FOUR: NEVER AGAIN!

1 Michael Miller, "'I Hated This Man More Than My Rapists': Woman Confronts Football Coach 18 Years After Alleged Gang Rape," *Washington Post*, June 23, 2016.

2 Karen Given, "Brenda Tracy Fights Sexual Violence, One Locker Room at a Time," *Only a Game*, WBUR, January 23, 2016.

3 Richard Boothman, "Fifteen + One: What (I Think) I've Learned," address at MACRMI (Massachusetts Alliance for Communication and Resolution Following Medical Injury) CARe Forum, Waltham, MA, May 7, 2019.

4 Paul Levy, personal communication, April 23, 2019.

5 Communities for Restorative Justice website, https://www.c4rj.org.

6 Denise Pena and Lorie Brisbane, "Victims and Justice Reinvestment in Oregon," *National Survey on Victims' Views of Safety and Justice*, 2016.

7 Paul Guzzo, "Hulk Hogan Returns to the WWE After a Three-Year Suspension," *Tampa Bay Times*, July 16, 2018.

8 Molly Howes, "The Power of a Good Apology," WBUR *Cognoscenti* blog, October 11, 2018, https://www.wbur.org/cognoscenti/2018/10/11/me-too-how-to-apologize-molly-howes.

9 Kathryn Schulz, *Being Wrong: Adventures in the Margin of Error* (New York: HarperCollins, 2010), 14.

10 Elisabetta Povoledo, "Pope to Host Abuse Victims Individually, Seek Forgiveness," *Boston Globe*, April 26, 2018.

11 *Globe* Editors, "Pope Makes Good First Step on Clergy Abuse," *Boston Globe*, May 11, 2019.

CHAPTER 8. THE AFTERMATH

1 Esther Perel, *The State of Affairs: Rethinking Infidelity* (New York: HarperCollins, 2017).

2 D. W. Winnicott, *Playing and Reality* (Abingdon-on-Thames: Routledge, 1991).

3 Rachel Howard, "Lent: Letter of Recommendation," *New York Times Magazine*, March 17, 2019.

4 Stephen Covey, *The 7 Habits of Highly Effective People* (New York: Free Press, 2004).

5 Belinda Luscombe, "World's Most Shocking Apology: Oprah to James Frey," *Time*, May 13, 2009.

6 Cris Beam, "I Did a Terrible Thing. How Can I Apologize?" *New York Times*, June 30, 2018.

7 Aaron Pratt Shepherd, "For Veterans, a Path to Healing 'Moral Injury,'" *New York Times*, December 9, 2017.

8 Arthur Brooks, "Our Culture of Contempt," *New York Times*, March 3, 2018.

9 "Michael Gulker: Conflict and Christian Leadership," interview by Faith and Leadership, Leadership Education at Duke University, January 22, 2019, https://faithandleadership.com/michael-gulker-conflict-and-christian-discipleship.

10 Kathryn Schulz, *Being Wrong: Adventures in the Margin of Error* (New York: HarperCollins, 2010).

11 Susan Fairchild, personal communication, February 12, 2019.

12 "Michael Gulker," interview.

13 Greg Taylor, "Fail Fast, Fail Often," Medium, October 17, 2018, www.medium.com/datadriveninvestor/in-silicon-valley-one-of-the-maxims-is-fail-fast-fail-often-4cacc447f30b.

14 Center for Teaching and Learning, Stanford University, "The Resilience Project," Student Learning Connection, accessed

September 27, 2019, https://learningconnection.stanford.edu/resilience-project.

15 Harold Stevenson and James Stigler, *The Learning Gap* (New York: Summit, 1992).

CHAPTER 9. WHAT ABOUT THE APOLOGY RECIPIENT?

1 Eve Ensler, *The Apology* (New York: Bloomsbury Publishing, 2019).

2 Farah Stockman, "The Crucial Act of Forgiveness," *Boston Globe*, December 25, 2012.

3 Tim Herrera, "Let Go of Your Grudges. They're Doing You No Good," *New York Times*, May 19, 2019.

4 Renée Graham, "Forgiveness Is Strength," *Boston Globe*, January 1, 2017.

5 Alexander Pope, "An Essay on Criticism, Part II" (1711).

6 Anne Lamott, *Traveling Mercies: Some Thoughts on Faith* (New York: Penguin Random House, 2000).

7 Graham, "Forgiveness."

8 Van Jones, *The Redemption Project*, CNN, 2019, www.cnn.com/shows/redemption-project-van-jones.

9 Paul Boese, "The Weekly Digest," *Droke House, Inc* 53, no. 8 (February 19, 1967).

10 Stephen Dubner, "How to Optimize Your Apology," *Freakonomics*, episode 353, October 11, 2018, http://freakonomics.com/podcast/apologies/.

11 Travis Anderson, "Hearing to Resume on BU Rape Case Plea Deal Left Judge 'Baffled,'" *Boston Globe*, April 10, 2018.

12 Fred Thys, "Former MIT Student Apologizes to Assault Victim for 'In-

excusable Behavior,'" WBUR *Edify*, April 10, 2018, https://wbur.org
/edify/2018/04/10/samson-donick-plead-guilty-rape-case.

CHAPTER 10. WHEN *NOT* TO APOLOGIZE

1 *Alcoholics Anonymous* (*The Big Book*), 4th ed. (New York: Alcoholics
Anonymous World Service, 2001).

2 Kwame Anthony Appiah, "The Ethicist," *New York Times Magazine*, January 20, 2019.

3 Kwame Anthony Appiah, "The Ethicist," *New York Times Magazine*, December 16, 2018.

4 Carolyn Hax, "Tell Me About It: Knowing How to Respond to
Overreactions," *Tampa Bay Times*, July 11, 2018.

Index

Index

Index

Index

Index

Index

Index

Index

Index

Index

Index

Index

Index

About the Author

Molly Howes, PhD, is a Harvard-trained clinical psychologist and an award-winning writer. Following a clinical fellowship at Harvard Medical School, she completed her doctorate in clinical psychology at Florida State University and a postdoctoral fellowship at Harvard Community Health Plan. Dr. Howes has led or contributed to research projects studying the interpersonal effects of depression, the impact of a parent's cancer on the child's psychological well-being, and the incidence and prevalence of mental health disorders in primary care practices and in larger populations. For thirty-five years, she has maintained an independent psychotherapy practice in which she sees couples as well as individual people of all ages.

Her creative nonfiction and essays have appeared in the *New York Times* "Modern Love" column, the *Boston Globe Magazine*, NPR's *Morning Edition*, WBUR's *Cognoscenti*, the *Bellingham Review*, and other literary journals. Her work received a Notable listing in *Best American Essays*, and she's the grateful participant in retreats with A Room of Her Own and residencies at the Virginia Center for the Creative Arts, Ragdale, and the MacDowell Colony.

Dr. Howes lives in the Boston area with her husband and visits the Gulf of Mexico every chance she gets.